The Book of Peace

# The Book of Peace

## MEDITATIONS FROM AROUND THE WORLD

### Claire Nahmad

JOURNEY EDITIONS
Boston • Tokyo • Singapore

*This book is dedicated to my mother, May Nahmad, for living a valiant life.*

First published in the United States in 2003 by Journey Editions,
an imprint of Periplus Editions (HK) Ltd., with editorial offices at
153 Milk Street, Boston, Massachusetts 02109.

Library of Congress Control Number: 2002116371

ISBN 1-58290-066-3

DISTRIBUTED BY

North America,
Latin America & Europe
Tuttle Publishing
Distribution Center
Airport Industrial park
364 Innovation Drive
North Clarendon
VT 05759-9436
Tel: (802) 773-8930
Tel: (800) 526-2778
Fax: (802) 773-6993
info@tuttlepublishing.com

Japan & Korea
Tuttle Publishing
Yaekari Building 3F
5-14-12 Ōsaki
Shinagawa–ku
Tokyo 141–0032
Tel: (03) 5437-0171
Fax: (03) 5437-0755
tuttle-sales@gol.com

Asia Pacific
Berkeley Books Pte Ltd
130 Joo Seng Road
#06-01/03 Olivinc Building
Singapore 368357
Tel: (65) 6280-1330
Fax: (65) 6280-6290
inquiries@periplus.com.sg

First edition
03 04 05 06 07 08 09    10  9  8  7  6  5  4  3  2  1

AN EDDISON•SADD EDITION
Edited, designed and produced by
Eddison Sadd Editions Limited
St Chad's House, 148 King's Cross Road
London WC1X 9DH

Typeset in Joanna MT and La Figura using QuarkXPress on Apple Macintosh
Origination by United Graphics, Singapore
Printed by Star Standard Industries (PTE Ltd), Singapore

# Contents

# Introduction

Peace is a precious gift we can give to ourselves, for our own health and healing and, wonderfully, to others as well. Peace is achieved within. By finding that point of silence in the sanctuary of the inner self we touch the source of deep healing peace. Once we have realized this transforming truth, we can all be peacemakers. We can all contribute in a highly significant and practical way to the establishment of world peace.

We can do this by using the act of meditation to harness two of the greatest powers contained within ourselves: the power of the imagination and the power of the will. By 'imagination' I do not mean the faculty of day dreaming or fantasizing, but the true creative power of the spirit within from which all art and culture spring, and from which we dream the potent dream before it can become reality. From the humblest to the highest objectification, everything in our world emanates from this point of creative consciousness. By 'will' I do not mean the blinkered self-will, which is the cause of so much conflict, but the higher or divine will.

To use our meditative power in the service of peace, we need to create images of peace through which its essence and vision can flow. When we do this regularly, as an aspect of our way of life, a beautiful miracle occurs. Spiritual teachers and seers tell us that the individual can indeed contribute significantly to the establishment of world peace. The flow of healing peace from the individual heart goes out into the world and permeates the consciousness of those who exist in chaotic conditions – both outwardly and inwardly – and helps to lift them into a dimension of being in which peace can begin to flourish. Negotiations and treaties can be pursued and effectively implemented at the practical and political level only when the hearts of those involved are ready to be receptive to this in-flow of peace.

Our prevailing philosophy is to think of peace as a negative condition, as 'lack of war', 'lack of conflict' or 'lack of strife'. But when we touch its heart-centred source, we realize that peace is a dynamic force, a revelatory path, a powerful state of being in which the loveliest garden of evolving human consciousness can take root and blossom.

This book contains eleven meditations from different cultures around the world, culminating in one global guided visualization that draws all the cultures together in a unifying meditation for world peace. From Buddhism to Native American belief and from Christianity to New Age thinking, each culture offers a guided visualization rooted in its own beliefs and traditions that leads you to an archetypal place of calm. By following each one you can enter into your own meditations for peace and, on emerging, give forth the closing affirmation in the form of a prayer. Each affirmation is an act of self-giving from the heart, combined with the higher will (the 'will to good') and the creative imagination. These three centres of power offer a beautiful way to serve the cause of peace. Your positive affirmations send personal messages of healing energy to the world to promote harmony.

# Guide to Meditation

To the beginner, meditation can seem quite a difficult concept to grasp. In our culture, which discourages the use of the imagination, activity is equated with being busy and outwardly productive. So the idea that the attainment of complete stillness of mind and body is an activity seems to the modern mind completely absurd. The further suggestion that there is a life deep within our consciousness far more vital, significant and beautiful than that of the domineering and organizing intellect beggars its narrow belief system.

However, if we are to create a sane world, a universal human response to values that create happiness, peace and fulfilment, and a kind, even-handed society, we need to believe in the practice of meditation. This should not be difficult when we observe the fruits of this most profound and powerful activity.

## The power of meditation

Proper meditation, practised with regularity and discipline, can transform one's life. The insights we gain, the health of mind and body we receive, and the daily renewal of soul and spirit that is the blessing of meditation will guide and revivify us in every waking and sleeping moment. Meditation is a cup that never runs dry.

The art of meditation may seem elusive at first. You are sitting there doing absolutely nothing, absolutely nothing is happening, and there are at least one hundred other things that you feel you ought to be doing, or would rather be doing, than sitting there trying actively to do nothing. This is the lower mind, or the everyday intellect, speaking to you. It will do everything in its power to persuade you that meditation is a foolish idea, and that you can put it off until tomorrow, or next week, or any time that is not now. (It always is 'now', of course!)

The lower mind has a tendency to drive us like cattle. It knows instinctively that once you begin to contact your higher mind regularly it is going to lose status, and so it fights frantically to gain ascendancy over your decision to meditate, filling you with feelings of urgency, guilt and frustration to 'act' instead. It will transmit to you all kinds of illusions, such as that you simply cannot meditate or that meditation feels uncomfortable.

Ignore its ranting, and remember that its impressions are pure illusion. Meditation is real, and the nagging voice of the lower self will soon be silenced by your quiet decision to continue with your efforts to meditate.

## Preparing to meditate

It is simple to learn to meditate, but it is not easy. Sit comfortably with your spine upright and supported if necessary. (If you lie down, you will almost certainly fall asleep, which is not a form of meditation!) Place your right ankle lightly over your left, because this seals your energy field, and cup your left hand in your right. At a spiritual level, we give with our right hand and receive with our left.

Having made sure that you are comfortable and relaxed, begin to focus softly on your breathing, drawing and releasing each breath imaginarily through your heart-centre. As you inhale, imagine that the golden light of the spirit is filling you. As you exhale, breathe out all the toxins, all the troubles and disturbances, all the dis-ease, from your mind, body and emotional self. Eventually, usually after a minute or two, you will find that you are 'in the light' and 'of the light', and you will naturally both give and receive the light in your breath-cycles.

Now think of the highest plane you can conceive of, and give this sphere an image. You may choose the figure of Christ or the Buddha, the Goddess or the Archangel Michael, Vishnu or Krishna. Or you may prefer a bright candle flame, the Sun or the six-pointed star (which resembles the Star of David but has no internal divisions). Whatever symbol you choose, it must be meaningful to you and symbolize Divine Intelligence.

As you hold this image in your mind's eye, you may like to softly chant the word 'Ham' as you breathe in and 'Sah' as you breathe out. In ancient Sanskrit, *Ham* means 'I am' and *Sah* means 'Higher Self', 'Divine Spirit' or 'Divine Spark'.

### Let intruding thoughts pass away

Your everyday mind will repeatedly attempt to sabotage the meditative process. When it makes its assaults by trying to drag you back to outer consciousness with some mundane thought or anxious rumination, simply return all your attention, with firmness but also with great respect and gentleness, to focus once more on your chosen image and the steady rhythm of your breathing and chanting.

Let your intruding thoughts be as boats that pass under the bridge of your mind. Don't jump on to them or watch them sail away; simply let them float by. Some of the thoughts that occur are merely distracting, but others occur purposefully for your healing and cleansing. Gently let all of them go, refusing involvement or feeling-ruffles of any kind. Alternatively, you may like to give these thoughts to the image of the Divine that you have chosen to hold in your mind. Let them rise up to your image of Divine Intelligence, to be taken care of by the supernal spheres.

## Attaining a state of calm

Soon you will reach a place of utter peace and calm, beneath and beyond the busy traffic of your thought processes, the biblical 'peace which passeth all comprehension'. It is at this point that eventually the spiritual worlds will open up to your inner vision, and your meditational journeys will begin, perhaps only for a second or two at first.

If even a split second of vision or breakthrough is beyond your reach initially, refuse the temptation to abandon meditation in disgust or despair! Your breakthrough will indeed come, the door will open before too long. This is incontrovertible cosmic law. It is just a matter of persistence in your practice of meditation.

## The purpose of guided visualizations

To start you on the meditative path, this book contains eleven guided visualizations of varying lengths, inspired by different cultures, which will stimulate your power to create images and enter into imaginal dimensions. In these visualizations you will be led to archetypes of peace and healing, such as the Lake of Peace, the Spiritual Mountain Top, the Garden of Delights, the Sacred Cave (meditation eight) and the Temple of the Sun.

Guided visualizations are a form of sacred storytelling that has a purpose for the listening soul beyond mere entertainment. The famous philosopher and psychologist Carl Jung recognized that the human need for integrating story was as urgent as the need for food, water, sleep, companionship and sex, and that the need for story provided evidence that we have a soul-existence as well as a physical one.

## Following a guided visualization

To do a guided visualization, sit in a relaxed and comfortable position for reading, keeping your spine as straight as possible and resting your right ankle on your left. Try not to slouch, as this greatly inhibits the depth and value of a meditational experience. Focus on your breathing, drawing and releasing each breath through your heart-centre until you are 'in the light' and 'of the light' (*see page 10*), then begin reading.

The act of reading, when undertaken peacefully in solitude – or at least in a state of withdrawal and detachment from immediate surroundings –

enables the reader to enter into a light meditative state, which is all that is required to fully experience the guided visualizations in this book.

If you are unfamiliar with meditation, simply follow the thread of each guided visualization to its end. In time, when you are more familiar with the practice of meditation, moments will occur during the course of a guided visualization when you wish to pause and follow your own path, seeking enlightenment from the voice and the imagery of your own spirit. This is when the real task, the true journey that is meditation, begins.

### Sealing the chakras

When finishing a meditation, even a light reading meditation, it is essential to protect your finer vehicles, your non-physical bodies, by sealing the chakras. These are inner gateways, power points in the physical body, where we are yoked or connected to the spiritual forces without which our bodies and the whole physical sphere could not exist.

To the eye of the psychic, the chakras look like spinning discs arranged in circles of petals like a rapidly rotating flower. In fact, they are perfect representations of a galaxy, which is also shaped like a spinning disc, with its stars, satellites and planets arrayed like the bright circling petals of a flower. It is interesting to consider what galaxies might actually be in the divine scheme of things, and to perhaps glean why the idea of a garden is sacred to all mythical and religious traditions, and is often given a cosmic dimension within them.

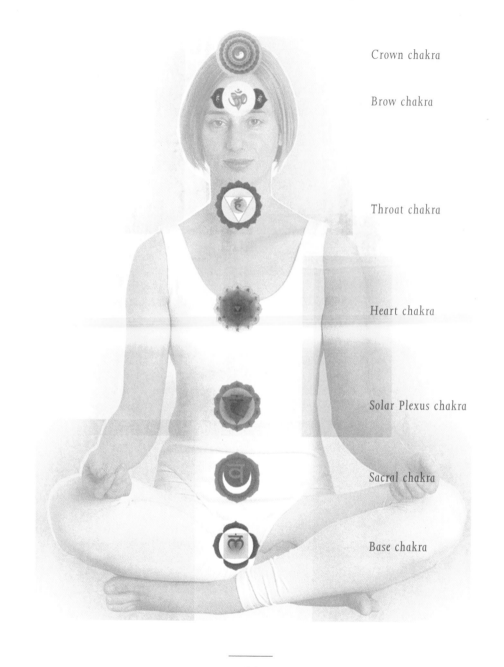

Crown chakra

Brow chakra

Throat chakra

Heart chakra

Solar Plexus chakra

Sacral chakra

Base chakra

There are many chakras, but the seven main 'stargates' we need to seal after meditation or any other spiritual exercise are situated in our corporeal body at the crown, the mid-brow, the hollow of the throat, the heart, the solar plexus, just below the navel, and the base of the spine. Imagine a vivid silver cross in a circle of light, and seal each centre by placing this symbol at midpoint upon each chakra in turn as soon as you emerge from meditation.

In most cases you will only need to seal the first five chakras (crown, brow, throat, heart and solar plexus). If you have entered very deeply into the experience, it will be necessary to seal all seven. You can also earth yourself by stamping both feet lightly on the ground. (If you do this heavily, you will shock your centres.) As you do so, hold the thumb and forefinger of the right hand together and say firmly on the in-breath 'I am' and on the out-breath 'present'. Do this three times.

### Affirmations for peace

Among the most important parts of these guided visualizations are the affirmations that appear at the end of each one. After you have completed the sealing and grounding exercises, sound the affirmation given to enhance the benefit of the meditation for yourself and for the world.

It is customary in many cultures to dedicate the fruits of meditation to all sentient beings. When you make this your declared intention before meditating, the affirmations that you give to bring peace to humanity and the Earth are increased in their influence and power.

# The Sacred and Eternal Flame

For this meditation you are asked to prepare yourself for a spiritual
journey to Tibet. You will project yourself by means of your creative imagination
deep into the Himalayas, where you will penetrate the secret recesses of a holy
mountain in order to learn from Buddhist wisdom the simple and beautiful
mystery of life itself. In this lies the secret of enduring peace.

## thoughts from tibet

| Angelus Silesius | Lin Hua Yong | Buddha |
|---|---|---|
| No man shall ever know what is true blessedness<br><br>Till oneness overwhelm and swallow separateness. | Without beginning, without end, Without past, without future. A halo of light surrounds the world of the law. We forget one another, quiet and pure, altogether powerful and empty. The emptiness is irradiated by the light of the heart and of heaven. The water of the sea is smooth and mirrors the moon in its surface. The clouds disappear in blue space; the mountains shine clear. Consciousness reverts to contemplation; the moon-disk rests alone. | There is only one moment in time when it is essential to awaken. That moment is now. |

# the contemplation

Buddhism cannot be defined strictly in religious terms. Buddhism is a perception and an awakening of the spirit to the nature of truth, or Divine Reality. It offers a practical philosophy for everyday life, which, so often exasperating and humdrum, is the magical pathway to the stars that sets our spirit free.

The Buddha taught that there were four Noble Truths.

The first of these is that all life is suffering. By this he meant that until we realize that our true nature is to strive to attain oneness with our Higher Self or God, we will be trapped in a world of material illusion in which we will be distressed and unfulfilled, unable to find peace no matter how much we satisfy the appetites of our physical, mental and emotional, sense-centred selves.

The second is that suffering is caused by selfish desire.

The third is that desire can be overcome, which ends suffering.

The fourth Noble Truth is that entry into Nirvana (perfection or paradise) and freedom from the great karmic wheel of life and death on Earth, in which we incarnate, die and reincarnate over the span of many ages, is to be won by following the Eightfold Path throughout life. The Eightfold path is composed of Right Understanding, Right Thought, Right Speech, Right Action, Right Livelihood, Right Effort, Right Mindfulness and Right Concentration. The last three elements are concerned with the practice of meditation.

The Buddha's Path is free from dogma or authoritarian strictures. In its concern for individual spiritual development, it reflects the precepts of the prophesied worldwide religion, which will appear at some point in the future. This religion will be concerned with the realization of the spiritual nature of the individual and therefore of the Higher Self or Divine Essence.

The Buddha was born Prince Siddharta Gautama in what is now southern Nepal, some 500 years before the Christian era. Deeply disturbed by the contrast between his opulent lifestyle and the suffering beyond the palace walls, he assumed the yellow robe of a pilgrim and searched long and hard for truth.

After subjecting himself to a period of asceticism, the only result of which was near death from starvation, he decided to take the 'middle way' between the extremes he perceived around him.

He bathed, ate and slept, and then sat beneath the boughs of a fig tree to meditate. After many patient hours, he emerged transformed, having received enlightenment and become an 'Awakened One' (Buddha).

One of the loveliest stories about Buddha is that which tells how he was persuaded to stay and help ailing humanity rather than leaving the chaotic Earth behind for ever. According to the story, Buddha was just about to ascend into Nirvana, having freed himself fom the karmic wheel, when he spied a tiny gnat dancing before him. The gnat was suddenly devoured by a hunting bat, and Buddha was so filled with compassion at the hapless creature's plight that he vowed to remain within the Earth's energy-field until every creature upon it had achieved enlightenment and thereby freed itself from suffering.

Esoteric lore says that he is with us still, helping and guiding us, and emanating his aura of compassion and loving kindness to all sentient beings.

# the guided visualization

Sit comfortably, spine upright, supported if necessary, and breathe quietly and easily, a little more deeply than usual. Imagine that you are in a great monastery, ancient and sacred, deeply sequestered within a naturally formed hollow in a mountain. You are being led by one of the Elder Brethren to a most holy place. Feel the worn smoothness of the stone corridors beneath your feet and the rougher ridges of the walls as you brush past them. Hear the faint echoes of bells and distant chanting – a reassuring, soothing sound.

Your guide leads you to a chamber, in the centre of which stands a simple altar. The altar is fashioned from the living rock and enshrines a single flame – the Sacred and Eternal Flame, which is the mystery of all life, all creation. You are ushered into its presence. You sit comfortably before the altar, and in peace and reverence you meditate upon the flame. Your guide withdraws silently, but you can feel his protective presence nearby.

The flame burns steadily, steadily, never flickering, never growing less. It is still, perfect in shape like two hands held, peaceful and poised, in prayer. Its colour is white, shining white, alive with a wonderful vibrancy, which is happiness, which is peace, which is blessedness.

Now the Sacred and Eternal Flame reveals its deepest secret to you. Your vision is withdrawn into your inner self. You see your own heart like a small cave. Within the cave burns the pure white light, the Sacred and Eternal

Flame, which is the source of your being. You know that in the heart of every man, woman and child there burns this perfect white light.

Now say the words of the healing chant, the Secret of the Flame:

'I meditate deeply upon the Sacred and Eternal Flame, which burns in my heart. I know that it is the pure essence of all life, all being, all creation. I know that it burns in the heart of every man, woman and child. Within the heart of all creation burns the Sacred and Eternal Flame.

'I now affirm everlasting brotherhood with all people, with all sentient beings, with all life, with our beautiful planet Mother Earth. The Sacred and Eternal Flame is the essence of divine and universal love, and it has the power to overcome every problem of my mind, my heart, my soul and my life. The white light of Love is healing, restoring, and beautifying every atom of my mind, body, and consciousness. I am in the light and the light is all.'

Now let the flame in your heart flower into the shape of a perfect six-pointed star that shines eternally above you in the spiritual skies. These are the celestial realms that lie within our own consciousness, not the physical skies of Earth. Meditate upon the shining, six-pointed star. When you are ready, descend to Earth again, safe in your ring of light. Seal your chakras with the bright silver star encircled by a ring of light, and make the affirmation.

### affirmation

I am enfolded within the heart of peace;
I am enfolded within the heart of love;
I am in the light and the light is all.

# The Spiritual Mountain Top

When life's uncertainties make you afraid, take the steps given in this visualization
to release your inner radiance and ascend to the archetypal mountain top, where your soul can
gaze out on the lovely vistas of the spiritual worlds and enter into the true meaning of peace.
Let the visionary myths of Japanese Shin-to guide you in their beautiful measured steps of
parable and story to the shining truth of your own being, its source of enduring peace.

## thoughts from japan

| Joy Kogawa | Traditional Shin-to Prayer | R.D. Laing |
|---|---|---|
| Flower Arranger | | The Bird of Paradise |

Among the weedy steel structures
And frenetic flowering of factories
I found a blind flower arranger
In a sketch of a room,
Dipping a drop of water
On to an opening petal
Of a tiny not quite flowering bud.
With his fingertips
He placed gentleness in the air,
Touching the air
With his transient dew.

When my eyes see some uncleanness,
let not my mind see things that are
not clean.
When my ears hear some uncleanness,
let not my mind hear things that are
not clean.

I have seen the Bird of Paradise, she
has spread herself before me, and I
shall never be the same again.
There is nothing to be afraid of.
Nothing.
Exactly.
The Life I am trying to grasp is the
me that is trying to grasp it.

# the contemplation

This meditation is inspired by the beautiful Shin-to (from the Chinese *Shen Tao* – the 'Way of the Spirit') belief system, the nature-religion of Japan. Within the tradition of Shin-to are the myths, fables and ceremonies that embody the timeless wisdom of the ages concerning the origins of humanity, its spiritual essence, its destiny and destination, and how that mystical destination is to be sought and won.

Shin-to teaches that natural forms are the dwelling places of divinities, their animating spirit. These spirits or 'kami' have two souls or activating principles, one gentle and creative – 'nigi-mi-tama' – and the other violent and destructive – 'ara-mi-tama'. According to Shin-to, the centre of balance for these opposing forces lies in human consciousness, that heart-understanding which aspires to purity and good.

Shin-to does not perceive of good and evil in sanctimonious terms, but rather as the success or failure of the unifying principle, the 'I', to harmonize the opposing dynamics of creation. When the 'I' is successful, the Sun Goddess Amaterasu is released from her 'cave' (the heart) and the light shines in full flood.

When the 'I' is unsuccessful, Susanoo the Sea God (symbol of the emotions and the stormy lower nature or ego) invades the expression of consciousness, causing ruin and terror with his depredations. As Japanese myth portrays it, Susanoo 'vomits in the holy places and defecates in the temples'. This graphic metaphor aptly describes how the incursions of the lower self into the arena of life, which properly belongs to the higher nature, dissipates the divine light and destroys peace, harmony and happiness.

In the same way that our lower, animal, natures are not evil, Susanoo is not considered evil, rather as overtaken by the power of ara-mi-tama, which leads to the expression of evil as an outcome, frightening the 'I' into shutting up its light and remaining hidden. In addition to symbolizing the heart, Amaterasu's cave represents the dark prison of materialism, where the untrusting, insecure ego locks its divine light away in the dungeon of selfhood. Blind to the reality of the spirit, and therefore refusing it permission to give out its radiance, the ego causes death, destruction and stasis to reign in the individual life and on Earth.

In Amaterasu's story, the gods use a mirror to coax her out of her cave. The mirror represents the 'I', the sphere of the being that is not complete without its four aspects – the soul, the flame of spirit, the harmonized and enlightened lower self, and the awareness that its individuality is sourced in a higher intelligence that unifies all beings.

When this mirror reflects Amaterasu's light back to her so that she becomes aware of it, the 'I' and its soul, channelling the light of the spirit, go forth together to climb to the mountain top. They are guided by the Bird Who Shows the Way, the wagtail, which in Japanese legend is mystically associated with the divine ancestors of the human race.

Lit by the lamp of Shin-to, Japanese Buddhism conceived of Amida Buddha, the beautiful 'Buddha of Infinite Light', whose paradise – like the Mystic Isles of Chinese religious belief – was in the enchanted West. Amida Buddha brought encircling peace and consolation, embracing all who called upon him. Through Amida, Amaterasu's light can shine undimmed for ever.

# the guided visualization

Visualize your heart-centre and gently make it a focus for your breath. Draw your breath easily and smoothly 'through the heart', breathing a little more slowly and slightly more deeply than normal. Still your body and your mind with the gentle rise and fall of your breath, keeping your spine straight and relaxed, supported if necessary.

You are standing upon a floating bridge, peacefully sailing across the heavens. The bridge is made of drifting cloud and thin, transparent vapour. These trails of cloud sometimes obscure the world beneath and sometimes flee dreamily from pools of shining twilight, revealing a land composed of many islands below.

There is a large central island upon which the surf pounds in spuming thunder. A little way inland an immense mountain capped with virgin snow rears its head into the sky.

A great majestic crane flies solemnly past you, moving slowly but steadfastly towards his mate, who sits waiting on an enormous nest at the top of a withered tree.

'We are weary of these shadows,' he says to you as he passes. 'Our eggs will not hatch in this half-light.'

'How long have you been waiting?' you ask the poor bird. He seems to sigh as he says upon the windless air, 'As long as I can remember.'

The floating cloud bridge upon which you are standing begins to lower itself until its curling vapours touch the rocky terrain leading towards the foot of the great mountain. You step off the cloud on to the ground, and at once the misty bridge disperses and disappears into the dusky air.

On the lower slopes of the mountain, above a natural terrace, you can make out the dark aperture of a vast cave mouth. You are drawn towards this opening, although it is clear even at this distance that a massive boulder completely obstructs the entrance.

It is an easy climb to the cave mouth. As you mount the terrace you feel as though you are still floating on air, even though you are aware of the sturdy rocks beneath your feet.

You stand before the mighty boulder blocking the entrance to the cave, and lay your hands on its smooth, mossy surface. For some unknown reason you long to go within, and it is as if your wish vibrates through your palms and into the huge rock.

You feel a tremor and sense the resonance of deep, rich laughter. Then a voice speaks from inside the rock: 'Why not ask me to grant your wish, child of semi-vision?'

In wonder, you request that the way be opened for you. Immediately, the stone rolls back a little, so that a crevice the size of a door appears at one side. 'Go within, and you shall see what you shall see,' the voice within the boulder murmurs, cryptically.

You pass into the gloomy interior. The cave winds ahead towards a distant glimmer of light. The broad corridor is grey in this strange interior gloaming, as if lit by ghost-candles.

You turn unexpectedly into a great echoing cavern. Mysterious subterranean winds moan within its contours like soft phantom voices, only just audible. On the left of the vast space there is a huddled shape that is twinkling and shimmering, emitting light.

You approach this starry enigma in fascination. As you draw near, you see that its luminescence is casting a fugitive, spectral light over the cavern walls, so that they glisten with a thousand breathtaking colour rays, shooting and flashing from a treasure encrustation of jewels, crystals and precious stones.

The light the figure throws out is very strange. A vivid, vermilion, intense splendour, the light seems as though it must burst out into firmamental glory but instead it is suddenly sucked down, weighed under, blacked out and reimprisoned by some sort of cloak, from which it re-emerges again and again according to the irrepressible necessity of its essence.

The startling realization comes to you that the cloak that holds back the light is composed of fear.

You sense that the figure needs your help and move closer to it. You see what appears to be a young woman who is too frightened to move, although the light that emanates from her reveals that she is a being of the

*The cloak that holds back the light is composed of fear.*

---

spiritual realms. 'Is my brother still outside?' she asks you. 'My brother dese-crates the holy places. Oh, the terrible pounding of the sea!'

You suddenly know that you must give your own heart-peace to this distressed goddess. You take her trembling hands and gently breathe forth the shining peace of your spirit.

As you give of your inner peace, your own human essence, the fear in the goddess subsides. Healed by the loving ministrations of a fellow being, she rises to her feet, her face radiant, full of renewed hope. 'We have a journey to make,' she says.

*f your inner peace, your own human essence, the fear in the goddess subsides.*

Together you walk out of the cavern and back down the passage towards the boulder that covers the entrance. The goddess speaks to the boul-der and it rolls right away from the cave mouth, out on to the terrace. At the same moment, a pied wagtail alights on it.

'We must follow the wagtail,' remarks your companion. As she speaks, you see a ray of light shoot out over the sea and hang there like a sword. It has come from beneath the goddess's cloak. She seems to shudder as she looks out over the sea.

To encourage her, you take the first step out of the cave, and she follows you into the dreaming twilight, glimmering now at its edges with a soft, silver light. The wagtail flies on ahead and you let it lead the way. You realize that you need to continue to encourage your dallying companion, who still trembles within her cloak.

Together you begin to climb the mountain, with the sound of the crashing breakers at your back, the pied wagtail going on before you.

You come to a spring, and the goddess stoops to wash her face and drink. When she rises again, she points in joy to a dim spot some way ahead in the unlit air. 'Look!' she cries. 'Look at the holy man!'

You can see nothing, but the mind in your heart prompts you to wash and drink from the spring too. When you raise your head you can clearly perceive a robed Buddhist monk, taking a peculiar route up the mountain. Instead of following the path as you and the goddess are doing, he is moving up its outer edge, rounding every jagged point, risking every precipice. Sometimes he seems to disappear altogether, and you fear he has fallen, but he inevitably reappears before very long, cheerful and chanting happily.

You and the goddess run to catch up with him and walk a little way with him. He greets you warmly, full of smiles. Then, suddenly, he is gone and you see him a moment afterwards, kneeling in a bare stony place overhung by great loose rocks. A sheer drop descends to the boulder-strewn beach below. He takes a vial from his robes and seems to give it to someone. Then, in a flash, he is back at your side.

'Will you not tread our way up the mountain?' asks the goddess. The monk respectfully replies, 'Honourable One, your way is the straight path, but I have taken that road already. Now it is my joy to take a different route up the mountain.' As he speaks he diverts suddenly to walk a treacherously slippy slope towards the spot where a man lies groaning. The monk bends over him tenderly and administers his vial. The man stops frowning and sits up, seeming to master his pain.

A wave of loving compassion moves towards the groaning man from the heart of the goddess. Receiving it, the man struggles to his feet, takes a deep breath, dusts himself down and sets off on his own path, which is below yours and less steep.

The monk beams with joy, bows reverently and then is off again with his vial to some other hair-raising spot. As you and the goddess continue on your path, he raises his hand in salutation. You notice that the cloak of the goddess has thinned and that the light at the edge of the clinging dusk has taken on a gleam of palest gold.

Next, you come upon a group of stately trees. Their lovely ethereal spirits are dancing in a ring upon a green sward, and you stop to dance with them. Moving in their circling dance is like becoming a moon or a star, wheeling gently in eternity.

As you take your leave and move on, you see that the goddess's dark robe is now even flimsier, and a flush of rosy light has appeared within the glow of pale gold along the frontiers of the twilight.

The wagtail continues to lead the way, progressing in little bursts of rapid flight and then settling so that you can follow, his tail bobbing and his eyes shrewd and bright. You are approaching the top of the mountain now, where a carpet of snow, alive with darting diamonds of light, lies over a small plateau that forms its peak.

Here stand eight god-stones, huge and round, as if fallen from heaven. The goddess takes her place among them and looks out over the thrashing sea. She beckons to you to stand by her side.

*Here stand eight god-stones, huge and round, as if fallen from heaven.*

The stones begin to sing and to speak in rhythmic chanting tones:

'Listen to the lesson of the stones, for it has been granted to you that you shall see and you shall hear.

'Children of Light, know this; that the world without is solely a vessel and a receptacle. Its only reality is that which you give it from your own heart, your own divine consciousness. The world without may sometimes seem sad, dreary, lifeless; it may seem unpalatable, squalid and pointless in its imperfect existence. When through fear, dismay or judgement you enclose yourself within the darkness of your own limited being, the world without becomes all these things, and you suffer greatly, and perhaps impose suffering on others. Indeed, the universe, always in resonance with you, must suffer in sympathy.

'But when you bring peace to the conflict, peace to the fear, peace to the dismay, peace to the judgement that chains and abuses your soul and holds it in darkness, the light of the spirit shines through your soul and makes all the world new.

'Now the world that so disgusted you is suddenly full of beams of opportunity to express your god-self, beams of joy, beams of laughter, beams of marvellous possibility that dance through your vision like a throng of radiant spirits from the celestial spheres. The grand tides of the life-giving spirit roll in majesty through the dimensions of your world once again.'

The goddess covers her eyes with her hands and repeats the words she spoke to you in the darkness of the cavern. 'My brother desecrates the holy places. Oh, the terrible pounding of the sea!'

The stones hum and vibrate with a strangely comforting reverberation. 'You were born to reign supreme over your brother,' they tell her.

'He will not obey you of his own volition, but obey you he must when you express the principle of your true essence. It is done by the magic of the breath, by going within and finding the point of peace hidden in your heart, by breathing out from there the rays of the heavenly light that loves and heals all creation.'

Listening to their words, the goddess reaches to her breast to unclasp the cloak that is fastened there. At once the wagtail flies to her, takes the loosened cloak in his beak, and wings far across the sea with it.

There is released such a beauty and an ecstasy of light that you are caught up in it entirely. You feel your heart-centre open of its own volition and radiate like the sun.

———

*You feel your heart—centre open and radiate like the sun.*

A moment later, you find that you are alone upon the mountain top. The snow has gone, birds are singing, wild flowers bloom in the crevices of the god-stones, and the sky is enchantingly blue overhead. The entire landscape is wreathed in sunshine, in blossoming trees, in bird and insect song.

At a little distance, the cranes' dead tree has sprung into life and has quickened into a crown of spring-green leaves. From their secretive depths comes the sound of nestlings calling to be fed. Overhead, the cranes wheel and dip in joy before swooping off in search of food for their young.

And the sea, the great plain of the sea, is still and blue and peaceful, calmly reflecting the sparkling sun and the azure heavens.

The goddess speaks from inside your heart, for she has gone within and is your centre:

'By my command, my brother the sea has transformed the savage beast that sprang in him. No more will he swamp and bring ruin to the holy places.' Behind you, the stones sing and rumble and oscillate. They speak directly to you:

'Child of unfettered vision, know that the sea is your emotional nature. Mighty it is, powerful and leaping with the life-force. But it is made to obey your heart-light, your Higher Self, and if it is not commanded by that self it will destroy all around it.

*Know that the sea is your emotional nature.*

---

'You enter the darkness to learn how to unite and free your sacred heart-light, and if you seek to liberate yourself from your prison by focusing on that divine centre, then you will assuredly be released before long. But do not despise the darkness. It has much to teach you, and is full of treasures for the spirit, the Higher Self.

*The goddess you rescued is your own soul who bears within her the flame of your spirit.*

'Know that the goddess you rescued is your own soul, who bears within her the flame of your spirit, for it is the soul who must locate the divine light and give it forth through your heart-centre.

'You have succeeded in your quest. You will always succeed in your quest. Be at peace.'

You sit down upon the soft flower-spangled grass and watch the beauty of creation, absorb the peace of the Invisible Presence upon the spiritual mountain top.

When you are refreshed and rested, let your consciousness descend into your place of meditation. Seal your centres (crown, brow, throat, heart, solar plexus) with the bright silver cross in a circle of light and earth yourself if you feel it necessary.

Now you are ready to make the affirmation of the spiritual mountain-top meditation.

### affirmation

My heart rests in quietude and ease, reigning supreme over my emotional nature so that all is peace.

My divine self shines out over the sea of my emotions, bringing comfort, bringing harmony, bringing deep heart-peace.

# The Spirit of the Rose

The rose meditation, inspired by the sayings of Christ and the insights of
Christian esotericism, offers a classic symbol that will bring you healing, ease of mind and
protection from the everyday onslaughts of existence. Let the mystical rose enfold you and
comfort you whenever insecurity or emotional pain disturbs your inner peace.

## thoughts from christianity

### Sarah Greaves

#### Peace is Within

Find the point of peace within.
It dwells not in the mind,
Not in the turbulent emotional body,
But deep in the heart, like a tranquil jewel.
Give up the haughty claims
of the mind,
Give up the anxiety-spell
of the emotional body;
Go straight to the heart.
Like a babe enfolded in the
embrace of its mother,
Peace will hold you in everlasting arms;

It is a rose softly lit with the light
of eternity.
Within its temple you receive
true Selfhood.
Your in-breath partakes of its holy essence.
You breathe out its fragrance to
heal the world.

### Rumi: Masnavi 1: 2022

Every rose that is sweet-scented is
telling of the secrets of the Universal.

### White Eagle

#### Spirit of the Rose

You have a great opportunity to work
for the upliftment and spiritualization
of the whole world, and for the
establishment of a universal
brotherhood in a world united and at
peace ... Brotherhood can only be
brought about by the spirit of the Rose;
and the spirit of the Son, Christ. Thus
we hold up for you at this time the
symbol of the Rose, this ancient symbol
of the Brotherhood, which is the
symbol of the heart.

## the contemplation

This meditation is inspired by esoteric philosophy drawn from the Christian tradition. The mystic form of the rose is linked with the human form. Except for one or two rare varieties, roses are built on a calyx of five sepals. A figure sketched around the sepals, joining their tips, forms a pentagram, the symbol of sacred proportion or the 'Golden Mean'. This is the point on a line where the smaller part is in the same proportion to the greater part as the greater part is to the whole.

Also known as Divine Proportion, the Golden Mean declares itself in every single line of a pentagram, which is itself the focus for magical seals and occult understanding, figuring most famously in the magic tablet used by John Dee, astrologer to Queen Elizabeth I, to invoke angels. The tablet was able to summon angels because it embraced the principles of divine balance, or heavenly peace, which is found in the heart of God from which all creative power flows.

The figure of the ineffable rose as the inner form of humanity inspired the Rosicrucians in their pursuit of spiritual insight and realization. A Christian mystical order, the Brothers of the Rosy Cross, understood that the cross was the symbol of a life of sacrifice lived within the four elements of Earth. At its point of intersection, the rose bloomed. From the earthly cross of time and matter there blooms divine consciousness in man and woman – the true spiritual essence of the rose.

A profound mystery resides in the emblem of the rose that blooms at the very heart of the cross: it is matter's innermost secret. The rose is a symbol of the heart and of human and divine love. When it blooms upon the cross of matter in an individual's life, the spiritual essence pervades the earthly being. In esoteric lore that man or woman is seen to be 'Christed', or expressing the divine life.

At the heart of every rose is a circle of golden stamens. It is a sigil, written in matter itself, of the 'mind in the heart', the seat of consciousness that is not the head-mind of everyday awareness or the limited, calculating, ego-rooted intellect, but rather the intuitive mind. Intuitive intelligence bears the gifts of inner seeing and spiritual percipience, within which can be found the true self.

This lovely symbolism is inherent in the Catholic Church's Golden Rose, a cluster of roses and rosebuds on a single stem, made of the purest gold and chiselled with exquisite craftmanship. At every benediction pronounced upon it, the Pope inserts a few particles of amber and musk in its cup among the petals. It is blessed on the fourth Sunday in Lent, and bestowed during the ecclesiastical year on a prominent woman within the Church whose religious devotion has exhibited itself through worthy deeds (the soul is perceived as feminine, and it is the qualities of the soul alone that can locate and quicken into being the mind in the heart). The rose is in this context a symbol of the Virgin.

It is said that a few minutes spent each day in meditation upon the heart of a rose will heal human ills and soothe every conflict and vexation of the spirit. There is a power and an essence distilled by the rose that is beyond all earthly understanding. Perhaps this is why Dante's highest vision was of the Celestial Rose of Paradise.

It is not always possible to meditate upon the heart of an actual rose. Yet we can enter the heart of the mystical rose whenever we wish to do so, and partake of the deep healing peace that is its essence.

# the guided visualization

Sit comfortably, spine upright, supported if necessary, and breathe quietly and easily, a little more deeply than usual. Bring before your mind's eye the image of a rose in full bloom. Our rose for this meditation is a pink rose, a deep rose-pink that is like the first flush of sunrise.

Think of the perfect form and structure of the rose, the soft radiance of its colour, its mystical perfume, the velvet and silk of its fragrant flesh. A rose is a being, a messenger from the angelic domains, visiting Earth to teach the wisdom, the truth, the beauty, the peace and the transcendent joy of life.

Begin to lay aside the garment of the physical body. Feel the buoyancy and airiness of your shining soul-body as it quickens with divine life. Your rose is before you like a light-filled temple formed from the mystic proportions of its glowing pink petals, a mandala calling you to go within.

Step into the rose, into that secret exquisite chamber. There is a pure and gentle radiance here, a tender and lovely power in the texture and composition of this rose temple. Sweetest of all is the enfolding fragrance, the rapturous perfume that is the spirit of the rose.

Touch the walls of the temple of the rose; kneel and touch the floor. It is like touching a welcoming hand, warm and loving, flesh made perfect, made divine. There is a source from which the radiance, the perfume, the body and the architecture of this sanctified being flows forth. Press deeper into the cave of the rose temple; walk on into its very heart.

Here at the sacred heart of the rose a precious, priceless jewel is shining. Lovely and beloved is that jewel so that your spirit dances as you behold it. Know that the jewel is your spirit, the laughing, singing golden and silver flame alight in your heart and in the heart of all humanity.

In wonder you watch as a golden door opens into the jewel. You step through this shining entrance into a chamber of rainbow light. At its centre is a seat of purest white light from which the seven lovely hues emanate.

There sits Divine Mother, Goddess of the Rose, smiling and welcoming you to her. In delight and adoration, you sit down at her feet and look up into her radiance to find that in her left hand she holds a distaff and is spinning, and with her right hand she is weaving ...

Folds and folds of the most delicate cloth fall away from her as she spins and weaves. It has a shimmering lustre, made as if by a flame dancing at the heart of a half-transparent pearl, and a swan's-down quality, like the silk of a spider. The magical rays of the rainbow play on and through it, for they are a living part of its weft. As you watch, sometimes it seems that shadows and mists gather, and darkness is woven into the cloth. Then you realize that the darkness always reveals a breathtaking treasury of brilliant stars.

In deepening wonder, you realize that Divine Mother is spinning and weaving the course of every human life down below so that the cloth contains a firmament of unfolding lives in its pattern.

Some souls encounter horrors and griefs that seem too great to be borne: it is these experiences that make the darkness in Divine Mother's cloth. Yet you see also that the arms of Divine Mother enclose every soul unfailingly, catching them as they fall, and that the arms of the Heavenly Father reach down to lift them into worlds of light.

Then the darkness melts away and is no more, for it cannot touch the children of Divine Mother and Heavenly Father. It has no real existence or dominion, and only descends for a measured time, until the bright star it secretes within its bosom is revealed to the encountering soul.

All this you see and understand from within the comforting shelter of Divine Mother, Goddess of the Rose. And deep within, where your heart's flame is at one with hers, you know with certainty that all is well, and that all manner of things shall be well.

As you sit at her feet, peacefully aware that your gentle breathing and the soothing rhythm of your heart draw their sustenance from Divine Mother, you see her heart-centre magically open like a golden flower that enfolds you, drawing you inside. You realize once again that you are in the heart of the mystical rose, cradled in golden light, hushed by the sweetness of Creative Silence, which lifts you on the swell of its grand symphony.

*You are in the heart of the mystical rose, cradled in golden light, hushed by the sweetness of Creative Silence.*

Heavenly perfume surrounds you and becomes your breath. As a child opening its eyes in the sun-flood of the morning, you see that all the

universe is a sphere, a perfect sphere of time, space and matter, kept perpetually in motion by the inconceivable fire which is the breath, the heartbeat of
God. And this sphere of matter revolves in the very heart of God, separated
only by a mist of its own unknowing.

Released from the spell of this ignorance, you dwell in the centre of
the golden light, aware that all around you is the great cosmic heart of love.
In bliss, in peace, you rest and have your being.

*All around you is the great cosmic heart of love.*

Then comes the Divine Child, the Golden One, the Christ, who is the
spirit of this perfect, all-enfolding love you are bathing in with such joy.
Receive his holy blessing; breathe in this miracle of deep, deep renewal,
borne on the breath of the Spirit of Love.

Know that love is the divine life, the inconceivable
fire, and that peace is its one true receptacle, its creative channel which alone can express the glorious dynamism of the
Godhead. This love, this peace, is given to you now.

Gently, you are led back, back to the house of your
physical body, back to the waiting Earth.

As you softly touch down into normal consciousness, you hear these words speaking in your heart: 'Let not
your heart be troubled, nor let it be afraid.'

Seal your centres and, when you are ready, make the
affirmation of the mystic rose of peace.

### affirmation

I am enfolded in the love and
peace of the mystic rose.
I am enfolded in the love and
peace of the mystic rose.
I am enfolded in the love and
peace of the mystic rose.

# The Tree of Life

Whenever your faith in life needs invigorating or material problems
threaten to obliterate your sense of peace and balance, turn to the shelter and
renewal of the omnipresent Tree of Life, which was conceived by the
mystic vision of ancient Judaic philosophers.

## thoughts from judaism

### The Old Testament: The Book of Psalms

#### The Twenty-third Psalm

The Lord is my shepherd; I shall not want.
He maketh me to lie down in green pastures:
he leadeth me beside the still waters.
He restoreth my soul:
he leadeth me in the paths of righteousness for his name's sake.
Yea, though I walk through the valley of the shadow of death,
I will fear no evil: for thou art with me;
thy rod and thy staff they comfort me.
Thou preparest a table before me in the presence of mine enemies:
thou anointest my head with oil; my cup runneth over.
Surely goodness and mercy shall follow me
all the days of my life:
and I will dwell in the house of the Lord forever.

### The Dead Sea Scrolls

#### The Parable of the Trees

One day the Trees of Life will put
forth a shoot which will become the
Everlasting Plant, for they take root
before they grow and extend their
roots towards the stream.
And the Plant will open its stem to
the living waters; it will become an
everlasting source of blessing.
All the wild creatures will graze
among its fallen leaves; all the
wayfarers will pass by its stem;
all the winged birds will nest
in its boughs.

# the contemplation

The Tree of Life meditation is inspired by the vision of the ancient Kabbalists, the esoteric interpretation of Judaism. Although not cited as such, the Tree of Life has always seemed to me to be a representation of the goddess, the sheltering, nurturing beneficent force that expresses the Divine Essence in form and links humanity's inner nature with the wisdom of physical nature as it manifests itself in the world.

The profound spiritual insight of the Judaic mysteries brought to humanity the concept of monotheism, the one supreme creator. Moses, the great prophet and founding father of the Jewish nation, is known as 'the world's first internationalist' and 'the most remarkable figure in the ancient world'. Although monotheism was rooted in Egyptian mysticism, it was Moses who, through self-sacrifice and obedience to his divine nature, lay the great cornerstone of Akhenaten's earlier vision. Some scholars and seers maintain that Moses was, in fact, a pharaoh with Jewish blood who, after he had been deposed and exiled because of his promulgation of monotheism, inspired the Hebrew slaves to follow him into Sinai so that he could establish his new religion within the protection of this sacred desert site.

The ardour, devotion and solemn religious majesty of the vision of Moses still moves through the music of the psalms and can be felt in other books of the Old Testament, in the Talmud and in *The Sefer ha Zohar (The Book of Splendour)* and *The Sefer ha Yetzirah (The Book of Creation)*.

According to the teachings of the Tree of Life, the Divine Essence split the atom of itself into male and female components, creating the evolutionary 'big bang'. This was done so that the Divine could realize Itself in a new way, and so that the Divine Being, the Adam Kadmon, could come into being. Everything that exists and is experienced by humanity as it progresses through its life on Earth can be transmuted to good, to creative building of the Adam Kadmon, if only it will learn the principle of balance.

Just as we have five digits on each hand and foot, divided and joined by the column of the 'tree-stem' of our bodies, so the tentacles of our senses and perception operate by working together in harmony. The number one has an upright symbol for the masculine principle and zero has a circular symbol for the feminine principle, the Divine Nothing. When these two symbols come together to form the number ten, numerals can progress in leaps and bounds.

The Ten Divine Attributes, known as the Ten Sefirot, are principles that must work together in balance and harmony so that the Creator may be 'returned to his Throne'. Everything in life must be balanced by its opposite principle. For example, justice without mercy is harsh and cruel and therefore does not adhere to Divine Law. Mercy without justice (or, more truly, wisdom) will bring about a state of life that permits abuse, leading to expressions of harshness and cruelty, which do not adhere to Divine Law.

The Angel of Peace is represented in the structure of the Tree of Life by the Pillar of Equilibrium. Equilibrium, or balance, is synonymous with peace. By reconciling within ourselves creation's dynamic and opposing life-forces, we will be able to find the point of balance, or the centre of peace, which lies within the mystery of the human heart.

# the guided visualization

Assume a relaxed meditative posture, making sure that you are comfortable and that your spine is erect and supported if necessary. Connect with your heart-centre, breathe gently 'through the heart' and feel your mind gradually becoming still and serene.

Begin to see a softly radiant angelic form take shape before you. It is a mighty angel, yet its presence is comforting and reassuring. It adapts its cosmic dimensions to the eyes of your soul, and you see that it is manifesting a female orientation.

Her robes are a cascade of white light over which the hues of the rainbow reflect and play in subtle shimmering tones, ever-changing in myriad variants of the seven hues. Look into her eyes, serene as blue summer skies, and let the realization wash through you that this is the Angel of Peace.

She takes you by the hand and you step forward out of your limited everyday self and slip away with her through the shining mists of dimension into the angelic worlds.

You have come to a celestial Earth, free from the constrictions of space, matter and time that encircle the physical Earth, which has passed away from your awareness like a shadow or a sigh or a fleeting dream. Now you behold the Earth of true reality.

It emanates such a flood of brilliant light that you can hardly register what you see before you until the angel begins to speak in a voice of calming quietude as soothing as the hush of fair-weather tides. She speaks directly to you and, as her words form, the light becomes lucid, and clear images rise and fall softly on your spiritual sight as she speaks:

*Come with me, Dweller in the Green World,*
*down into the deep secret places of the Earth, down deep into her heart.*

'Come with me, Dweller in the Green World, down into the deep secret places of the Earth, down deep into her heart. Here there is a great light, which glows like no outer Sun, but rather blazes with a spiritual light so pure and lovely that mortal eyes may behold it only in dreams and visions of the spirit. It is the brilliant effulgence of love and joy, the supreme radiance of the Divine.

'Here in the Earth's heart it is as if we stand in a paradise garden, and in the garden there grows a tree. It is the Tree of Life. We may go to it and stand at its great gnarled roots, which wind away in all directions like petrified serpents. How firmly anchored they are in the stuff of Mother Earth!

'Gaze up in wonder, Human Soul, into its fragrant boughs, garlanded in leaves tenderly glowing with a soft, peaceful green hue, and hung with fruits of heavenly, scintillating colours sparkling with the lustre of the stars. Rainbow-coloured birds come and go among its branches, as do little birds of gentle dun Earth shades, and strange mythic animals whose fabulous colour and form you have never seen or imagined before. Each one speaks to our heart and is our brother, our sister. In joyous communion we greet one another, and our voices rise in song, for it is the Morning of the New Day. Yes, the dawn is breaking and, as we look up, further and deeper into the mysteries of the Tree, we see that there exist many paths upwards into its winding boughs, as though it were all at once a tree, a mountain and our soul's deepest dream.

'In delight our hearts take wing because we see that, at its very summit, the Light of the great Spirit streams forth and pours downward like a bright river of paradise deep into the heart of the Earth where we stand, into our own heart vessels and into the world of sorrow below. Do you not see, Human Soul, that this great Tree of Life has roots not only at its base but also at its crown, and that these crown-roots are nourished by supernal worlds

*Do you not see, Human Soul, that this great Tree of Life has roots not only at i by supernal worlds which may seem to you to vibrate at a measureless distan*

which may seem to you to vibrate at a measureless distance, but which I tell you do not lie far beyond but rather embrace the physical Earth?

'Now in a vision within a Vision, we see ourselves moving upwards upon two of the paths that lead from the roots, up to the heavens where the Shining Ones that you call angels choir in a wonder of bliss to inspire us on our upward way – yours to struggle in a tomb of flesh, ours to inhabit a radiant atmosphere pulsing with creation's joy. There is a beautiful reason that this is so, and through it a triumph to be won that is beyond imagining.

———

'Do not wonder, Earth Child, on beholding that path parallel to your own. It is the path I tread, the beauty-path of the angels, for just as we descend from the heights, so must we also ascend again. Angels too have a path of evolution blessed by the Tree. We are always with you and we can share worlds whenever you reach out to us and seek our presence.

'With the Staff of Life, the Pouch of Provisions and the Undying Lantern we climb, and we are never alone. Around us, everyone upon their own elected path, we see the sons and daughters of Humanity and the sons and daughters of Faery ascending likewise. The path of Faery is a never-ending dance of the Earth's delight, for your feet also if you will tread it. Your paths cross and interweave. Fairy, angel and human beings are all linked in a network of light. And see how the birds of the Tree alight and dart and give forth music! They know no thresholds, but are dwellers in all three spheres.

ase but also at its crown, and that these crown-roots are nourished ut which I tell you do not lie far beyond but rather embrace the physical Earth?

'Now we are alone again, with the peaceful Tree stretching above us waving its beautiful branches over our heads in benediction. Soothed, we pause to dwell upon the wonderful shelter and protection it offers us, its kindly power and strength, the motherly perfume of its fruits and flowers, the lullabies in its rustling leaf-songs.

'Look carefully, Human Soul, for ten ineffable blossoms of the beautiful mystical rose are beginning to appear upon the Tree. Notice that within each exquisite formation of fragrant petals is a winged figure.

Together they are the Ten Divine Attributes of the perfected ManWoman, known as Adam Kadmon.

'Ponder these things, for the secret of the winged figures at the heart of the blooms is of liberation and peace for all creation.'

The Angel of Peace falls silent, and you see that she is becoming absorbed into the Tree. You understand that in a sense she is the Tree, its great supporting dynamic, and you realize that the essence of the Angel of Peace is balance. She balances all the Ten Divine Attributes upon the Tree, and that is why she is truly the Angel of Peace.

In deep quietude, she gives you her blessing.

Refreshment of soul and gladness of heart steal over you. You stroke the bark of the Tree and feel its goodness, its wholeness. Rest contemplatively beneath its spreading green boughs for a while and consider the teaching that the great Angel of Peace has offered to you as her gift.

Balance in all things is the secret of peaceful living, for all suffering is a deprivation of balance. You realize that the Tree, with its great temple-like pillars, balances all creation and that every soul is given the opportunity to express the sacred principle of that Golden Mean of perfect balance. It has only to desire to do so.

*The Tree of Life is also the Tree of Peace.*

You look again upon the Tree of Life, and see the Angel of Peace as a quiet pulse emitting her essence from its heart. The revelation comes to you that the Tree of Life is also the Tree of Peace.

Comforted, healed and ready for renewed service, you seek once more the mundane Earth of physicality below, taking with you the vivifying Light of the New Day.

You feel the solid ground beneath your feet, slowly refocus upon the things that surround you, and seal your centres. You are now ready to make the affirmation of the Tree of Life.

### affirmation

All the help I need to balance my inner
and outer life is available to me.
I only have to ask to receive it.
The Angel of Peace is in my heart
and builds her temple over me.
The roots of the Tree of Life are ever
at my feet and at my crown to give
me strength and peace whenever
I need to draw on them.

# The Enchanted Fairy Isle

When the pressures of life overwhelm your ability to find and enter the peace
of your own inner world, let this visualization guide you gently within so that
you may discover tranquillity, recuperation and clarity once again.

## thoughts from celtic mythology

*Anonymous*

### The Enchanted Isle

To Rathlin's Isle I chanced to sail
When summer breezes softly blew,
And there I heard so sweet a tale,
That oft I wished it could be true.
They said, at eve, when rude winds sleep,
And hushed is ev'ry turbid swell,
A mermaid rises from the deep,
And sweetly tunes her magic shell.

And while she plays, rock, deli and cave
In dying falls the sound retain,
As if some choral spirits gave
Their aid to swell her witching strain.

Then summoned by that dulcet note,
Uprising to th' admiring view,
A fairy island seems to float
With tints of many a gorgeous hue.

And glittering fanes, and lofty towers,
All on this fairy isle are seen;
And waving trees, and shady bowers,
With more than mortal verdure green.
And as it moves, the western sky
Glows with a thousand varying rays;
And the calm sea, tinged with each dye,
Seems like a golden flood ablaze.

They also say, if earth or stone,
From verdant Erin's hallowed land
Were on this magic island thrown,
For ever fixed, it then would stand,
But, when for this, some little boat
In silence ventures from the shore –
The mermaid sinks –
hushed is the note,
The fairy isle is seen no more!

## the contemplation

Celtic mythology, with its Star Goddesses, its wildly beautiful and fantastic imagery, its potent Earth Mother and the great father figure of the Dagda is beginning to be recognized as significant and seminal a source as classical mythology. Certainly the profound imagery dwelling magically within the chronicles of King Arthur and the Knights of the Round Table have won worldwide acclaim.

The Druids formed the priesthood of the ancient Celts. Both male and female in number, it is now believed that the Druids were not the fearsome and bloodthirsty cult described by the Romans, who were eager to destroy the power of the mystic priesthood, but were an enlightened and humane religious order who practised vegetarianism and healing as well as magical arts.

After the natural death of the body, the Druids ritually buried the head at a sacred site. By preserving the seat of consciousness. the Druids believed that the departed soul could return to occupy it and speak to diviners. The ritual was also performed for practical and sanitary reasons. It would have been impossible to bury entire bodies in great numbers at their holy sites, and the head, in addition to being the part of the body most closely associated with individuality, was subject to minimal putrefaction compared to the remainder of the corpse.

Christ, during his period in the wilderness, is reputed to have come to Britain to learn from the wise and kindly Druids, who were said to have advised him concerning his ministry and final earthly destiny, as well as teaching him their knowledge. The Greek philosopher and mathematician, Pythagoras, who advocated vegetarianism and perceived the working of divinity in mathematics, was also said to have been influenced by his visits to the Druidic priesthood.

Brigid was the most deeply venerated goddess of the ancient Celts. Her name, pronounced with a silent 'g' (Bri–h–id), gave rise to the modern English word 'bright'. She was goddess of fire and the stars, of poetry and artistic inspiration, of music and song, of compassion and women, of purity and love. She was also keeper of the greater destinies, goddess of prophecies and dreams, of the fairy peoples and of the mystic western isles, conceived of in numerous religious traditions. Her emblems are the lamb, the dove, the dandelion, the rowan tree and the oyster-catcher, the seabird that uncovers pearls. In ancient times she was called 'the Shepherdess' by her worshippers.

The famous Celtic mystic, Fiona Macleod, says: 'I believe that though the Reign of Peace may be yet a long way off, it is drawing near; and that Who shall save us anew shall come divinely as a Woman – but whether through mortal birth, or as an immortal breathing upon our souls, none can yet know.

'Sometimes I dream of the old prophecy that Christ shall come again upon Iona; and of that later prophecy which foretells, now as the Bride of Christ, now as the Daughter of God, now as the Divine Spirit embodied through mortal birth – the coming of a new Presence and Power; and dream that this may be upon Iona, so that the little Gaelic island may become as the little Syrian Bethlehem. But more wise it is to dream, not of hallowed ground, but of the hallowed gardens of the soul, wherein She shall appear white and radiant. Or that, upon the hills, where we are wandered, the Shepherdess ... Brigid the White ... shall call us home.'

# the guided visualization

This visualization will take you on a journey of wonder deep into the heart of the Lands of Fairy.

Make sure that your spine is straight, fully supported if necessary, and that you are comfortable and relaxed. You are going to call upon a fairy guide, one of the Handmaidens of Brigid – Goddess of Fairy, Woman of Compassion, Healing and the White-golden Light of the Higher Essence – who will usher you into her holy presence.

Breathe a little more deeply and a little more slowly, 'through the heart', and feel the enhanced magical quality of the airs of Fairy as they begin to flow around you.

An enchanted door appears before you. It is arched and made of oak, medieval in design, and studded with gold and silver.

*An enchanted door appears before you.*

The door swings open. Beyond, there is a starry twilight haze.

You hear your guide from afar, singing a song of wild loveliness as she approaches you, a high piping melody brought from the depths of the fairy worlds. Soon she stands before you on the threshold, smiling in greeting. Around her moves a swirl of violet and green mists from the Otherworld.

You move towards her, out of your earthbound self, and step into the shimmering twilight beyond the oak door. Your guide slips her right hand into your left and, as you link with her, you are given the gift of flight. You surge through the ethers at great speed, aware of stars and spinning worlds and shining mist. It is as though you are travelling through the Milky Way.

You and your guide come to rest upon wide sands that stretch down to a rocky shore, beyond which plunges a northern, blue-grey sea.

Its passionate waves give birth to white horses, where the billows become potent towers of jade wine, crashing into the fearful, jubilant body of the ocean with their white steeds of the soul. All about you is the boom, the joy and the spell of the sea and the song of majestic wheeling flocks of strange seabirds, making music of a deeper weeping ecstasy and a sweeter lamentation than those known on Earth.

Before you lies a huge spiral carved into the sands, like the impression left by some some great basking sea creature. Your guide leads you along its winding path to its sacred centre point.

As you reach the sacred centre, your guide lets go of your hand and recedes slowly into a perfect ring of bright light so vivid that at first you cannot register the being at its heart who is casting it. Then the dazzle is gently removed from your vision, and you behold Brigid, goddess of the human and the fairy worlds.

She is radiant with golden energy. There is about her something of a wondrous maiden softly clothed in the blue of heaven, and something of a tall, fair queen, angelic in her bearing, and something of a being more ancient than the stars, who scintillates with divine fire. Such is the power of her sublime beauty that sentient creatures can look on her only with adoration and wonder.

Brigid embraces you with her universal love and enfolds you in a cloak of her own golden radiance. She calls you by your name and says to you, 'We will journey together to Hy-Brasail, the Isle of the Blest, the enchanted isle, which some call Tir-na-Nog.'

You find yourself standing alone again in the centre of the spiral traced on the beach, looking out over the rhythmically turbulent northern sea to the distant horizon. Suddenly, you become aware that a mysterious island is gradually appearing as if at the rim of the world, at first a blue haze far away, yet growing clearer and more vivid with each breath you take.

So lovely is this island, veiled and remote yet haunting as the presence of a dream, that you walk out to the very edge of the rocky shore where the running waves surge and retreat, as though you might walk through the tossing wilderness of the waters to reach it.

On the crest of a wave there bobs into sight a little round coracle, which finally comes to rest at your feet. It is so small that at first you are wary of stepping into it, but you hear Brigid's sweet, reassuring voice speaking within your inner ear, and take heart.

'Have no fear. This little boat is built from the charms and incanta-tions of your heart's desire. You have built it well, and it will not fail you.'

You grasp the coracle and jump into it. The next great wave sweeps you away, and you ride on the summit of the waves in exhilaration until you reach the glimmering shores of the fairy isle.

As you disembark, you notice that evening has fallen and that the great sun is making glory on the waves and beginning to sink in a lake of crimson and orange fire below the rim of the western world. Brigid whispers within your heart that you have come to the Isle of the Blest, to Tir-na-Nog, Land of the Ever Young. She tells you that this island is the jewel of the enchanted western isles.

Turning from the splendour of the sunset-bright ocean, you see that that this land is indeed fair and gracious, bathed in a loveliness that never shone over any mortal world.

It is a magical twilight world of soft dusk and starlight, and you see that it is inhabited by the noble fairies, the Sidhe, who move in shining, opalescent garb, weaving magic and influences, which they dispense to the dim Earth far away.

Their task is a delight to them, and you perceive that they dance and feast on rare fruits and magical foods drawn from the rays of the quiet starlight all night long under the glittering constellations. Everywhere there are lovers, engaged not in physical conjoinment but in their own created currents of ecstasy, and this in turn is given to the Earth, and to other planets that spin in the material cosmos in the remote soul-distance.

You think of the wheeling Earth and of the energies of Nature as they are expressed in her verdure, our own green world, and you understand the source of their ardour, the sweet eroticism of their giving forth. You ponder on these things, knowing they are marvels.

You are approached by a fairy couple strange and majestic in their exquisite pulchritude of form and face and aura. These are the Prince of Tir-na-Nog and the Mistress of the Realms, a woman powerful and mighty in her fairy sphere, graceful as a willow wand.

You know them. You know who they are and that a mutual glad familiarity exists between you even before they greet you. With few words they invite you to join the fairy feasting and dancing.

You are ready to partake of their moonlight revels, and the hours of the night fly by on dancing feet as swift as your own. Once or twice you are guided by the invisible presence of Brigid to look into the bowered glades between the trees. There in the soft moonbeams you behold the marvellous sight of the kings and queens of fairy dancing as in a charmed dream with a host of noble unicorns, white as the foam of the wave.

In the morning, the sunrise over the sea is greeted with undimmed delight by the fairy people of the enchanted western isles because age, weariness and broken dreams cannot approach them. On the Isle of the Blest, in the Land of the Ever Young, you rejoice with them, and receive the unalloyed peace and blessing of the dawn.

After the sunrise celebrations, the Prince of Tir-na-Nog and the Mistress of the Realms lead you to a natural bower richly festooned with fragrant woodbine and wild roses. They seem full of animation and excitement, as if something magnificent is about to be revealed.

They tell you that Brigid came to them last night in the ceremony of the unicorn dance and instructed them that you are to be anointed with the Three Fairy Mysteries, called the Jewels of Peace by the fairy peoples.

The knowledge comes to you, like a bird flying to its perch in your mind, that the Sidhe, the noble fairy hosts of the inner worlds, are truly the People of Peace, pronounced by ancient lore older than the Earth to have the sacred Jewels of Peace in their safekeeping, which they will vouchsafe to heart-centred mortals.

You look deep into your own heart-centre and see there a flame burning, golden white, ever radiant, inextinguishable. As you begin to comprehend the profundity of the honour to be bestowed on you, the quintessence of the gift to be given, that seed of light, which is the flame within your heart, kindles into a star.

---

You see that it is the nature of a star to perpetually and abundantly give forth its own essence. The realization comes to you suddenly that when you have received the Jewels of Peace from the fairy peoples, you will be able to continually give of them to others.

The Mistress of the Realms and the Prince of Tir-na-Nog take you through the woods towards the peak of a Visionary Mountain that glimmers at a spectral distance. As the trees recede, you are led to a clear shining lake lying between miniature hills, which are clad in a pelt of smooth green grass and moorland flowers. Here, the spirit of the lake, the fairy queen Olwen, rises from the waters to greet you.

Free-hearted, laughing, Olwen invites you to bathe in her magical lake, to absorb the beauty of its sweet wildness and loneliness and to wash away the clinging bonds of trivia, superficiality and artificiality of the mundane earthly world, which send the soul to sleep and close the heart like a sun-deserted flower.

You accept Olwen's invitation and bathe in her sanctified lake. Immediately you feel the descent of soul-calm and spiritual renewal, which make the springing waters of your inner being as limpid and light-filled as the mirroring expanse of Olwen's wild pool.

As the waters wash over you, there comes a sudden rush and beating of wings, and seven white swans fly in formation around the lake. They come

*You bathe in Olwen's sanctified lake ... feel the descent of soul-calm and spiritu*
*the springing waters of your inner being as limpid and light-filled as th*

*They come to rest upon its shores, and there they shed their swan garb and enter the water as seven fairy beings ...*

to rest upon its shores, and there they shed their swan garb and enter the water as seven fairy beings, beautiful maidens of brilliant radiance who sport and play in the body of the lake and who yet remain swans but are released from the constrictions of literal form.

Laughingly, they insist that you too have a cloak that shrouds your spirit. They tell you that in order to receive the first of the Fairy Mysteries, you must be prepared to shed this cloak, without shame or regret, just as they have shed theirs.

You ponder their words, perplexed, for you cannot see your cloak. The dullness of Earth has been washed away from you, but you are not yet a shining being as they are.

As if a spell had stolen over the lake, evening comes, and three constellations appear brightly overhead, twinkling through the dusk. They are the seven stars of the Great Bear, the constellation of the Little Bear from which the Pole Star shines down with a soft intensity, and the muted fire of the Pleiades, the lovely star group called the Seven Sisters.

Their reflections dance and shake and stream through the waters, and you know that your soul is earthing their spiritual electricity and absorbing the light patterns of their supernal currents.

*enewal, which make*
*irroring expanse of Olwen's wild pool.*

*You see Brigid appear like a sun-disc above the swan-maidens.*
*She holds a jewel that is like a cauldron of fire.*

The swan-maidens surround you, and gently remove a shadow that you permit to fall away from your vision.

You see a reflection of yourself in the water, but it quivers and swirls so much that you cannot bring it into lucidity.

Then you see Brigid appear like a sun-disc above the swan-maidens. She holds a jewel that is like a cauldron of fire. She anoints your forehead with three drops from Olwen's lake, and places the cauldron into your hands.

Instantly, the reflection stills, and you see that your hands are illuminated by the cauldron of fire, which catches light flowing from an incandescent spinning wheel located in your solar plexus.

'Place the Jewel within the wheel,' Brigid tells you. 'It is the first of the Three Fairy Mysteries, the first of the Jewels of Peace. Your hands are its symbol and its secret. It is the power to serve, your giving of yourself in service. The Jewel is kept bright by self-giving.

'That which is brightest within you must be discovered and must be given to others, in all circumstances of life. When you give forth the rays of this Jewel, which dwells within you, what you give forth will save you. If you do not give forth this radiance within you, then that which is within you will destroy you.

' This is the wisdom and the sacred knowledge belonging to the first Jewel of Peace.'

Wondering at her words, you place the cauldron of spiritual fire into the spinning wheel that lies within your solar plexus, your bodily centre. Immediately you fall into a healing, integrating sleep that lasts only for a breath of a moment.

When you awake, you find that the Prince and the Mistress of the Realms have lifted you over the beautiful grass knolls surrounding Olwen's Lake, and have carried you into a wide, flower-filled valley, above which the sun is at its zenith.

'This is the Place of Rainbows,' they tell you. 'Here you shall prepare for your next initiation.'

In this secluded vale, fragrant with delicate flowers of the wilderness, some shy, some wanton, your childhood self awakens and delights in the golden sunshine and the sweet vivid blue of the heavens, sailed by islands of fair-weather clouds, shining with a white angelic purity.

At the heart of the valley, the Fairy Woman Blodeuedd appears, she who is formed from flowers.

As fair as summer and as many-coloured, she plucks flowers from her own breast and, one by one, holds them in the rays of the sun, so that they express their colours and release their scent through the power of the sunlight as if through a great crystal.

She weaves the spell of their individual qualities in a series of healing incantations, so that their magic falls on you as a benediction.

As you receive the virtues of the flowers into your body and soul, Blodeuedd gives you the knowledge that there is healing in earthly plants and trees for every human ill, and that healing can be given to a human being not only by ingesting the physical essence of flowers but by absorbing the deeper quintessence of their beauty directly into the soul.

The Fairy Woman Blodeuedd begins to walk to the top of the valley and, as she walks, she draws a soft veil of gentle summer rain over the green flowering dale. At the head of the valley she turns and creates a living rainbow from the flowers she has used in her spells.

With a further incantation she lifts you up to its highest point, so that you are held in the prism of the rainbow, with its arch sloping before you and behind you down to the valley and, your intuition tells you, deeper still into the dimensions of the physical Earth from where you have made your long journey.

There you rest, poised in the radiance of your own higher self and in the rays of creation that reach the Earth from beyond the firmament. You are borne aloft and supported by the fragrance of the valley of flowers and its feminine spirit, which teaches you to aspire to the eternal peaks of the spiri-

*As you rest in the heart of the rainbow you become aware that it has become a great fountain, and that you are standing in its centre, which glows like a jewel, being caressed by the springing water.*

---

tual realms and to the Invisible Presence that walks there in mystery.

As you rest in the heart of the rainbow, you become aware that it has become a great fountain, and that you are standing in its centre, which glows like a jewel, being caressed by the springing water.

The Prince and the Mistress of the Realms are with you, bathing in the rainbow-coloured rays of the fountain.

Again, you watch yourself mirrored in the translucent drops. There you see the fountain springing within you, rising like a rose tree between your throat, brow and crown, joining the three centres of perception, and flowering in a measureless plume above your head. As you observe it, you see that it is a fountain, flowers, a tree and a rainbow, and that all are consumed and made one in an inconceivable flame of fire.

*You see the fountain springing within you, rising like a rose tree between your throat, brow and crown, joining the three centres of perception, and flowering in a measureless plume above your head.*

Brigid appears once more and stands in the fountain with you and your companions. Her golden presence gilds the flashing of the water and makes it dance with the blue of wild hyacinths.

'This is the Fountain of Youth,' she says, 'the threefold Jewel of Peace and the second of the Fairy Mysteries.' She anoints you with three drops of water from the fountain, and hands you the golden and silver branches of a living tree, which is hung with blooms of heaven's light.

'Place this branch within the flame of fire that is the Fountain of

Youth inside your being,' she instructs you. 'You can bathe there whenever you need to remember that you are eternally young.'

Brigid touches the hollow of your throat in blessing and speaks again. 'The secret of the branch is that it is from the Tree of Life. It governs your words, so that, in remembering the reality of these spheres of the spirit, you will not speak harshly or hopelessly. For does not your soul perceive here the beauty and nobility of the brotherhood of creation and all its members, and does not it bathe here in the everlasting joy of being, and know that all worlds must culminate in an expression of joy?

'Nor will you speak with judgement, for you have seen here that dimension gives birth to dimension, and worlds beyond worlds turn in the Creator's heart. Therefore with your words you will seek wisdom, but never judgement, and you shall have peace.'

You feel Brigid's touch in benediction on your brow-centre as she continues to speak to you.

'What you see and what you hear in your circumscribed Earth-world will never make you forget what you have seen and heard in the inner spheres of true reality, and thus you will see and hear differently to those who are enmeshed in materiality. Your eyes and ears will ever look beyond,

You will see and hear differently to those who are enmeshed in materiality.

hear beneath the masquerading illusions that blind and deafen those bound to the mortal world, so that you see and hear always an aura, an echo of deeper beauty, deeper meaning; and you shall have peace.'

Brigid finally places both hands in blessing around your crown-centre. 'The light of your perception will draw its breath, its inspiration, from the light you have found within, emanating from the mystery of the spiritual worlds. It will never enclose itself in the darkness of the intellect and the limited human mind.

'You will not elect to sit in a squalid prison, but will always make journeys and follow quests into dimensions blissfully beyond the heaviness and darkness of the Earth planes. What you perceive will ever dance joyfully in the radiance of your higher vision, and you shall have peace.'

'Your words, the windows of your eyes and ears, the doors of your mind, are all blessed, and all shall know peace.'

Your words, the windows of your eyes and ears, the doors of your mind, are all blessed, and all shall know peace.

As Brigid finishes her teaching, you place the golden and silver branch with its flowers of light into the Fountain of Youth that you carry within yourself. Immediately you do so, you fall into a reviving sleep for a fraction of a moment.

When you awake, you find that you are lying on a bank of soft grass at the very foot of the Visionary Mountain.

A train of noble fairies comes riding towards you, led by the Prince of Tir-na-Nog and the Mistress of the Realms, riding side by side. Between them they bring a riderless white horse shining with the beauty of the full moon on snow, its mane like a bridal gown and its hooves shod with the purest silver, full of darting lights.

*They bring a riderless white horse shining with the beauty of the full moon on snow.*

'This steed is Perillion, prince of the fairy horses of the Tuatha De Danaan,' the Mistress of the Realms informs you, smiling. 'He is for you. Mount, and ride with us!'

You see that Perillion wears a splendid silver saddle. You place your foot in the stirrup and straddle him with ease. On the back of your steed you feel mighty and majestic, valorous and invincible. The wind fills your hair and braces your lungs.

'We will ride to the mountain peak,' says the Prince of Tir-na-Nog and, at his command, the horses rear and prance and bolt up the grassy flanks of the mountain.

You ride with the others, in a race with the wind to reach the mystic mountain top. Perillion's pace and strength is magnificent, and you break through the white mists around the peak, the first to arrive.

Here it is a different world. There is a stillness and a calm which is deeply magical, and all around you stretch vistas of worlds, spheres and dimensions of unending glory and loveliness.

'This is the beginning of all the worlds, and the world's end,' says the

Prince, riding up behind you and looking out with you over the vast star-fields of Creation's light. 'Dismount and follow me.'

You follow his instructions and jump to the ground as the Mistress of the Realms rides up and also dismounts. She walks by your left side, and the Prince walks by your right, as the riders of the Tuatha De Danaan form a great circle around you, still mounted on their steeds.

Under a fruitful hazelnut tree lies the round rim of a well. It is at the topmost point upon the peak of the Visionary Mountain. You take your place at its edge, together with the Prince and the Mistress of the Realms, forming the three points of a triangle around the well-top's ring of stones.

'This is the Well of the Holy Chalice,' says the Mistress of the Realms; and like the answering chimes of a bell the Prince states simply, 'It is the Well at the World's End.'

You look down into the deep, deep well.

In here the stars are shining, not reflected but radiating mystical light from their own hallowed and ineffable dimension. Within the well swims a great fish, and you know that it is the Salmon of Wisdom, the oldest creature of all the worlds.

Into the depths of the well the Fairy Hazel, tree of wisdom, of the

This is the Well of the Holy Chalice ...
It is the Well at the World's End.

fire of the stars and the creative flame of the poetic imagination, drops its fruit. You begin to see Brigid reflected in the waters of the well. As you look into the blue of her wise and timeless eyes, you become the leaping fish, the Salmon of Wisdom.

Hazelnuts rain down into the well from the fruitful tree, and, as they touch the water, they break open, releasing the kernel within. In leaping joy, you swallow the fruit of the hazelnut tree, and pass into a sublime world where you are alone with Brigid.

'This is the Fairy Paradise that lies secretly at the heart of your Earth-world,' she says to you. 'It is called the Glen of Precious Stones.'

You look around, marvelling at the mystery of this exquisite place. Surrounding you are breathtaking landscapes, seascapes and starscapes, all formed of the most delicate-hued and spellbindingly beautiful crystals, gems and jewels. Beyond them, in the far distance, rise rock facets of liquid fire, as if fresh quantities of precious stones were perpetually being born. Their colours are an ever-flowing, ever-changing mandala of fantastically lovely patterns that rise and fall in eternally new tints and hues, following a tongue of joyous white flame, which seems to be their source and their creator.

'It is the flame of the heart,' Brigid tells you. 'It dwells here, in the heart of Fairy, which is the heart of the Earth-world, and in the heart of every being, and in your heart.

'You can pour the light of the precious crystal that is your heart into other human hearts, and into the energy patterns of the many Earths that spiral around the one perfect ideation, which is the template for all its myriad dimensions. You can pour the light of the crystal especially into the Earth that is your home.

'This perfect Earth must one day be expressed faithfully through all its lesser bodies, even that of your physical Earth, which is the darkest of all the Earth planes.

'This new age that will bring a perfected Earth into being cannot come about until the Enlightened Ones, who have received the knowledge of the Three Mysteries, join together and give of their heart-essence, their heart-light, consistently each day, so that gradually a great tide of sacred light will lift your Earth into a higher dimension.

'The breath is magical, and it is through the agency of the breath that the deed is done.'

Brigid teaches you how to simply and naturally breathe forth the sacred light from your heart-centre, so that it is given out in love to the spinning Earth beyond, and to all its creatures.

She stands by your side, and together you give out the sacred breath, the sacred light, to all the Earth.

---

*Give out the light.*

Together you give out the light.

Brigid takes you back into the waters of the well, where it seems as though you are floating among the stars. She anoints you with three drops of the well water, and takes a golden-white, six-pointed star from her breast.

'This is the third of the Fairy Mysteries, and the greatest of the Jewels of Peace,' she tells you. 'It is within your own heart already. I hold only its reflection. Nevertheless, place this Jewel in your heart-centre, and always see it clearly in your thoughts.

'Its six rays give out the sacred light, and its seventh ray is its centre point, its divine source, which takes the form of a mystical rose.

'The secret of the third Jewel is its power to transform, and its power to give of its highest essence without ever growing less. The more you use it, the more abundant it becomes.'

You place the last Jewel of Peace within your heart, and see it there ablaze with light, enshrining the rose at its centre.

The secret of the third Jewel is its power to transform, and its power to give of its highest essence without ever growing less. The more you use it, the mor

A half-second of sleep steals over you and, when you awake, you are standing at the threshold of the oak door you first came through. Brigid stands at your side. Your fairy guide is with her, waiting for you.

Brigid smiles in farewell and, lifting her cupped hands over your head, showers you with sparkling spiritual gold as though it were confetti. It is her gift and her reward.

Your fairy guide leads you through the arched door, back to your earthly place of meditation. She withdraws into her swirling mists of violet and green, and the door closes and vanishes.

Gently return to normal consciousness, still bathing in the fragrant golden sheen, which is Brigid's gift and which clings as softly as flower petals to your aura.

Seal your chakras (crown, brow, throat, heart and solar plexus) with the bright silver cross in a circle of light, and earth yourself if necessary. Now make the affirmation of the Jewels of Peace.

### affirmation

The Jewels of Peace shine out from my heart. I can give their magic to others.

I am clothed in golden shining light. The winds of misfortune and hindrance that blow in the outer world cannot disturb my deep golden dream of peace.

I carry the peace and the magic of the fairy worlds within my heart. Their calm replenishment feeds me whenever the vibrations of the physical world become distorted and discordant.

bundant it becomes.

# The Temple of the Sun

Whenever you face discouragement in your personal life or experience
feelings of hopelessness or helplessness concerning world affairs, seek refuge
in this meditation upon the Celestial Temple inspired by ancient Chinese
religious belief. The magical peace of the reflections of the *Tao Te Ching*,
and the beautiful tradition associated with the goddess Kuan Yin, will once
again enable you to give and receive peace and recognize the goodness
and worth of your life's path.

## thoughts from china

| Taoist Meditation | Lao-tzu |
|---|---|
| Close your eyes and you will see clearly. | The Valley Spirit never dies. |
| Cease to listen and you will hear Truth. | It is called the Mysterious Female. |
| Be silent and your heart will sing. | And the doorway of the Mysterious Female |
| Seek no contacts and you will find union. | |
| Be still and you will move forward | Is the base from which Heaven and Earth spring. |
| on the tide of the spirit. | It is there within us all the time. |
| Be gentle and you will need no strength. | Draw upon it as you will, it never runs dry. |
| Be patient and you will achieve all things. | |
| Be humble and you will remain entire. | |

# the contemplation

The religion of China has been largely misunderstood by the West. Its ancient form was a state of spiritual enlightenment, which incorporated elements of the Japanese Shin-to system of perceiving divinity in nature and natural forms (*see page* 23), and lay very close to much New Age and esoteric thinking of today.

The ancient Chinese did not worship their ancestors, but they did venerate them. They viewed their ancestors as Elder Brethren, souls who had gone on before and had attained a higher state of evolution than those still toiling in Earth lives, who were willing to offer help and guidance to their younger brethren.

The ancient Chinese understood the law of karma and reincarnation to the extent that borrowers of wealth or goods would strike deals to repay their creditors in their next life. An 'ancestor' was, properly, a soul who had transcended the need for incarnation and had ascended to the celestial worlds.

The progressive spiritual concepts which we are beginning to recognize and explore today were to the ancient Chinese absolute and practical realities. In the earliest history of Chinese civilization, women were deeply esteemed and honoured, and the golden pheasant – the earthly representative of the divine Fêng bird – was worshipped as their symbol.

The seminal ideas of ancient Chinese philosophy were those of Yang (male) and Yin (female), of manifesting Spirit and Law (Ch'i and Li). These concepts, rooted in their spiritual vision, inspired the system of ethics evolved by the sage Confucius and the mystical thoughts of his contemporary (some say pupil), the

Old Master, Lao-tzu. Legend has it that Confucius and Lao-tzu once had an inter-view, after which Confucius declared in exasperation that he could understand the flight of birds and the movement of fishes, but he could not understand Lao-tzu, and could only compare him with a dragon!

Lao-tzu's essence is enigmatic. His birth is said to have been miraculous. His teachings – the 'Tao' or the 'Way' – reveal how to perceive and be guided by the movement of spirit through the world of matter with the entire sphere of one-self rather than the intellect alone. This inspiration emanates from the feminine, Yin, principle of wisdom, which the more Yang-orientated, cerebral Confucius could not comprehend, so prompting him to liken Lao-tzu to the feminine dragon. In the *Tao Te Ching*, Lao-tzu bequeathed to the world an interpretation of that most enigmatic and profoundly subtle system of perception, the transcendental under-standing embodied in the Hindu *Upanishads*.

The tradition of Kuan Yin symbolizes the beautiful loving-kindness ethos of Buddhism. It is associated with the Chinese prophecy that a female Buddha will incarnate on Earth, embodying the compassionate Yin force without which the Yang principle becomes incapable of expressing the healing dynamism of peace.

# the guided visualization

Concentrate on your breathing for a few moments, quietly inhaling and exhaling. Focus on your heart-centre as though you are breathing 'through the heart'. Ensure that your spine is straight, relaxed and comfortable, supported if necessary. Through the simple rhythm of your breath, find the point of peace within, where all is calm and tranquil.

You are walking up a gently sloping hill to the doorway of the sublime Palace of Light. The palace has three tiers and is built of mirroring silver and flashing white gold, inlaid with purest pearls, white crystals and faceted diamonds. The craftsmanship of its construction is as delicate as exquisitely wrought lace. It pulses with lustre as if it were the lightener of the stars.

At either side of the arched doorway stands a beautiful Chinese woman in traditional dress. You exchange bows with both women before entering the Palace of Light.

As you walk into its interior you feel as though you are stepping into a vast fountain of pure brightness. Through the pearly rays of light you see that at the heart of this central chamber there is a great three-tiered altar of shining white marble.

Upon the top tier of the altar a great vermilion bird, with sweeping tail feathers and plumage of fiery beauty, sits waiting. It is the Chinese phoenix, the mythical Fêng bird. As large as a small horse, she sits with wings outstretched, regarding you with ocean-deep eyes, azure as blue jasper.

You kneel before the altar and dedicate the sacred flame in your heart to the spiritual source of light within the chamber, which is being broadcast to the world from the Palace of Light.

As soon as this is done, the mighty Fêng bird swoops to your feet. She invites you to climb on to her back so that she may become your aerial steed. Her feathers are long and silky, beautifully soft and warm. It is easy to cling to her without fear of falling.

She rises straight up into the air, like a skylark. As you gain height, the Fêng bird gives forth a rapturous river of song, and you both soar into a rarefied spiritual dimension far above the astral plane you first encountered.

There is another temple here, set on a hilltop in the supernal worlds, the perfect ideation of the Palace of Light far below. It is made of a living white substance more beautiful than any material essence. It constantly eases, cleanses and delights the soul, setting the bird of your spirit free so that it ascends and sings with the golden Fêng bird, which is now circling the roof of the temple in ecstasy.

You see the flame in your heart dancing within your spirit-bird, and a greater, more potent flame incandescent within the Fêng bird. You know that both are firebirds, manifestations of divine consciousness; and you understand why, in the legends, they are so precious and so sought after.

---

You enter the doorway of the temple, and see within a single white rose upon an altar like a still white flame forming a chalice, white as alabaster.

A venerable Chinese sage stands before the altar. He beckons to you to come forward. 'This is the white rose of peace,' he explains. 'Take its perfume into your own heart and breathe it out to heal the conflict in the hearts of humanity.'

*This is the white rose of peace ... Take its perfume into your own heart and breath*

You stand before the altar and inhale the pure fragrance of the rose of peace. Within its embrace the certainty rises within you that you are a being of absolute light. Your power of self-giving becomes supreme, universal.

Your in-breath receives and your out-breath gives. Breathe out the magical perfume of the white rose to every member of humanity.

As you give of your deepest and eternal self, you see the seeds of peace catching fire in the hearts of many receptive human souls across the Earth, which penetrates even these exalted spheres.

You observe that the cherished seeds of peace are active, pregnant with myriad possibilities. You understand that peace is a dynamic, ever-unfolding state of consciousness that will bear humanity on in the power of its free-handed giving to an inconceivably glorious destiny, individually expressed, omnipotent in its unity.

As the Chinese sage draws the peace-giving ceremony to a close, you are aware that within you its force lives on, and can always be given forth.

---

He leads you to an antechamber, which is like another temple, unbounded in its structure. You see before you gardens and magnificent wildernesses, hallowed and vigorous, which wind in and out of one another and are part of one another. There are mountainscapes and oceans, and a huge city glimmering softly with jewels in the far, far distance, hung with thin drifting mist-veils of blue and bridal white.

You wonder what this place can be.

The sage hears your unspoken question and says gently: 'My child, it is your own spirit home, your own temple. You have built this world within the inner scapes of your own heart, for therein lies the creative force. When you use your creative force to build, you give of the deepest essence of yourself and add to your celestial temple.'

He smiles and plucks as if from the air an immaculate golden flower, like a star and a lily, perfectly arrayed within as the petals of a yellow rose.

'Learn the secret of the Golden Flower,' he says as he places the exquisite bloom in your hands. 'Within, you contain a holy and most magical power, which you must learn to seek with a pure heart. Then you must learn to wield this power so that you may build, in the light of truth, translucent life and a translucent Earth – a life and a world that does not block and refuse the light, but allows it to express the brilliance of love.'

The ancient sage seems so beautiful in the soft light of the temple that you wonder if the Fêng bird is the shape of the flame of his spirit. Again, he catches your thought and looks up through the domed glass roof of the temple, where the two birds, the Fêng and your own spirit-bird, are still blithely wheeling.

'I will show you to whom the Fêng belongs,' he says, smiling at you mysteriously.

You re-enter the Temple of Peace and walk into its gardens, which open around you like an embodied joy. The Chinese sage leads you to a flowering peach tree, and prepares to take his leave of you.

'Before we part,' he says, 'I will give to you a simple jewel of truth. Never overlook the power of the word. It is mighty. When you need to find peace in your earthly life, make of the word "peace" a gentle, rhythmic chant.

You will be enthralled by its mystical power, for it will be as if you summoned a great Angel of Peace to heal and renew you.'

The sage gives you his blessing. You exchange bows, and he returns to the shining temple. As he enters it, the domed building seems to become a measureless winged disc, radiant as the sun. When you look down at your hands to study the golden flower the sage placed in your cupped hands, you discover that its image is now unmanifest, and you know that it has returned to rest in your heart.

In the bird-fluting quietness, you can hear the song of a swiftly running river.

In the bird-fluting quietness, you can hear the song of a swiftly running river. Within the music of its babble and laughter, you can make out tearful, sobbing sighs.

Leaving the fragrant dell where the peach tree grows, you mount the grassy bank before you and pass into a shallow river valley, where pastures of beautiful wild flowers, vivid and delicate, stretch to the river's edge.

The waters of the river are golden — a pale celandine hue where they run past you, and a deep and rich laburnum yellow in the winding distance.

A group of rocks, glowing soft and clear like amber, grow out of the river's margin like a wild and scattered monument. Upon this outcrop, a tall Chinese woman stands while the waters of the river lap her feet.

She is clothed in a high headdress surmounting traditional Chinese robes with flowing sleeves. Her figure is graceful and noble, and the radiant majesty of her face reveals that she is a goddess.

She holds a pitcher full of liquid, which she is pouring into the river. The pitcher is filled continually by her tears, which stream in crystal rivulets from her beautiful eyes.

Despite her queenly aura, you feel that the goddess is approachable. You walk to the outcrop of rock and ask her compassionately why she is so full of grief.

The goddess smiles through her flowing tears.

'Is not the sorrow of the Earth cast up in us so that we may heal it?' she asks. 'If you have sometimes known sadness, but have not known its cause, you too have shared in this work.'

As she speaks, her tears cease and a light leaps up from the golden river, casting rainbows through its spray as it surges over the rocks in its bed and through the last of her tears as they are shed into the pitcher and poured into the body of the waters.

'I am Kuan Yin, Goddess of Compassion,' she tells you, 'and my pitcher contains the balm I pour forth on troubled waters. This is the Yellow River, the River of Life, which flows forth into the physical world.

'How can it not bear sorrow on its breast? Yet that sorrow is the water that hollows a receiving chalice into the surface of the level stone. The chalice is created so that it may be filled with joy. When the purpose of sorrow is understood, its distress can be soothed into peace.'

Kuan Yin steps down from her rock, leaving her pitcher at the water's edge. 'I shall return to it, by and by,' she comments, 'but first you shall help me in another work.'

She takes your hand and leads you into an upward-sloping meadow, where you can see the blissful gardens of the temple unfolding in beauty as far as your vision can reach.

She takes your hand and leads you into an upward-sloping meadow where you can see the blissful gardens of the temple unfolding in beauty as far as your vision can reach.

———

'These are the Gardens of the Celestial Temple of the Sun,' she tells you. 'The Temple is the gateway to the Source, to the Everlasting Mystery that lies within the heart of the great central sun of your physical universe.

'These sanctified gardens belong to the Great Mother, Queen of Heaven, whom we call Si Wang Mu. Her holy spirit is everywhere! Under her divine authority, we shall perform a work of peace for your world.

*Under her divine authority, we shall perform a work of peace for your world.*

'I am a goddess of compassion, but also goddess of mercy, goddess of prayers. As an act of divine mercy, I shall summon all the prayers for peace from Earth's humanity which the Great Mother has received into her heart.'

As Kuan Yin falls silent, a tender breeze stirs and lifts your hair, spreading the robes of the goddess on the air currents and bearing with it the sweet incense of the gardens as an aromatic gift for your soul.

As if the fragrance sharpens your spiritual senses, you hear a keening, beating sound from the west, and, looking that way, you see for a moment the dim twinkling shapes of mystic isles, far out on the western sea, caught in a violet haze upon the ocean's blue rim.

'Behold! They come!' exclaims Kuan Yin, and there is song in her voice. Suddenly you are surrounded by an endless flock of pure white doves. They mass and circle above you, giving forth their sweet purring cries.

They form the shape of an arrowhead and fly straight into the heart of the goddess. You are astonished to see that, within the space of an intake of breath, they have disappeared.

---

Kuan Yin smiles at your wonder, and opens her arms wide, as if in compassion, as if in embrace, to the Earth-world, which spins in darkness and sorrow within the world of the garden, although somehow far below and beyond it.

'Help me to send these birds of peace out into your world, as messengers from the Celestial Temple of the Sun,' she implores you.

Commanding the birds from your heart-centre, speeding them on wings of light to their sacred destination, you aid Kuan Yin as the whirring flock of doves is released from her heart in the perfect formation of the white rose of peace. They fly far, far away, and as you watch you see them settle all over the world in benediction, like atoms of the Angel of Peace. They seem to fill the face of the Earth.

'Each one is a prayer offered for peace,' explains Kuan Yin in her musical voice. As you turn to look at her, you see that a few of the doves have not yet started on their journey, but are flying around both of you. As they swoop and flutter, the rays of the sun catch their plumage so that they shoot stars of white light out into the air.

Simultaneously, the doves each cast a shadow, so that shadow-birds also wheel around you.

Kuan Yin laughs in joy, saying, 'In my earthly country, we have a saying: You cannot stop the birds of sorrow from flying through your hair, but you need not let them nest there.'

You watch entranced as birds of sorrow, birds of joy, fly around and around your head, now shadows, now glancing light. At last, they too fly to Earth to become birds of peace.

'Our work is nearly done,' says Kuan Yin. As she speaks, the golden Fêng bird and your own little spirit-bird fly overhead. They make straight for the heart of the sun, and disappear into its incandescent disc.

'Have no fear,' says the goddess. 'Your spirit-bird will return to you, as my bird, the Fêng, will assuredly return to me.' As you look at Kuan Yin, you see that her traditional robes echo the style, grace and fluidic beauty of the fiery Fêng bird, which is the divine emblem of Kuan Yin and the Queen of Heaven.

Kuan Yin again takes you by the hand and you descend through the inner spheres until you are back in your place of meditation once more. Before she leaves you she shows you a dove nestling at your heart-centre. 'Remember that the Doves of Peace will descend on your soul at your command,' she tells you. Then, in parting, she throws the brilliance of her love and protection around you as you end your meditation.

Return to normal consciousness, seal your centres (crown, brow, throat, heart and solar plexus) with the bright silver cross in a circle of light, and earth yourself if necessary. Now make the affirmation.

## affirmation

I feel my pain so that I may be visited by joy.
My pain and sorrow is transmuted into deep soul-peace.
The pain and sorrow of the world is transmuted into abiding peace.
The Doves of Peace descend gently upon me so that I am immersed in a soft rainfall of healing peace.
I release the Doves of Peace into the heart of the world for its healing.

# The Lake of Peace

When the unsettling ripples of life's setbacks and disappointments threaten your peace of mind, or guilt and fear rise from the depths to haunt you, find solace in Vishnu's lake of perfect peace, 'sanctified as the clear mind of a devotee'. Let the spiritual magnificence of the Hindu vision enfold you with gentle serenity in a golden dream of peace.

## thoughts from hinduism

### Krishna: from 'Dialogue on the Soul', the Bhagavad Gita

I am the beginning and the middle and the end of all that is. Of all knowledge, I am knowledge of the Soul. Of the many paths of reason I am the one that leads to truth.

Of sounds I am the first sound, A; of compounds I am co-ordination. I am time, never-ending time. I am the Creator who sees all.

I am death that carries off all things, and I am the source of things to come. Of feminine nouns I am Fame and Prosperity; Speech, Memory and Intelligence; Constancy and patient Forgiveness.

I am the Brihat songs of all songs in the Vedas. I am the Gayatri of all measures in verse. Of months I am the first of the year, and of the seasons the season of flowers.

And know, Arjuna, that I am the seed of all things that are; and that no being that moves or moves not can ever be without me.

Know thou that whatever is beautiful and good, whatever has glory and power is only a portion of my own radiance.

But of what help is it to thee to know this diversity? Know that with one single fraction of my Being I pervade and support the Universe, and know that I AM.

# the contemplation

The great Hindu religion is fed by the mighty rivers of the *Vedas* (*Books of Knowledge*), the *Upanishads* (*Lessons*), the *Ramayana*, the influence of Buddhism, and the *Bhagavad-Gita* (*Song of the Lord*) contained within the *Mahabharata*.

The *Bhagavad-Gita* is the heart of Sanskrit literature and its eighteen chapters are recited and sung daily by Hindu devotees. They tell the story of the dialogue between the prince and pilgrim-warrior Arjuna (the higher mind or soul) and Krishna, the spirit. When Arjuna becomes dispirited and refuses to fight the battle, a symbol of the individual struggle to win and enter the Kingdom of Heaven, Krishna speaks the verses of the *Bhagavad-Gita* to him to encourage and strengthen him. Eventually, Arjuna agrees to 'fight the good fight' and Krishna becomes his charioteer, the spiritual force that carries him and spurs him on to victory.

Hinduism is defined by its respect for all creatures and the colour and spectacle it brings to its vision of the eternal verities. Its esoteric teachings, the *Upanishads*, instruct that the one true purpose of existence is to reunite the individual soul (atman) with the Universal Soul (Brahman), from which it was originally separated so that it might come to consciously know itself and Brahman. In so doing it would realize its essential unity and non-separateness with Brahman and with all the other 'individual' souls Brahman contains. The act of dividing, of individuation, is seen as a negative force of illusion necessary for this process of enlightenment.

The *Upanishads* reveal that wisdom is an intuitive understanding, a clairvoyance of the higher consciousness that can only be attained by the atman's complete surrender to the Universal Soul. It is a gift of Brahman and cannot be achieved through the expansion of the intellect alone, which is a gift of awareness, stemming from the ego or the lower self. Many spiritual teachers maintain that scientists will not make the necessary breakthroughs to solve the problems of existence on Earth until they let go of the assumption that reality can only exist in material terms and ascend into the knowledge of the Higher Self. Then all things (within the capacity of the Earth-cycle we are living through) will be made known to them.

The Katha *Upanishad* tells the story of Naciketas and his meeting with Yama, the Overlord of the Dead. Naciketas asks: 'Does a person continue to live after the death of the physical body?' Yama reveals that the path to wisdom is to be found through the practice of yoga, which brings quiescence to the mind and senses.

'When cease the five knowledges (senses), together with the mind, and the intellect stirs not – that, they say, is the highest course. This they consider as yoga – the firm holding back of the senses. Then one becomes undistracted. Yoga, truly, is the origin and the end.'

Krishna revealed to Arjuna the concept of karma yoga, a discipline of positive action in the world. He taught that this was a new way of releasing the soul from its cycles of reincarnation because it is not the acts people commit in themselves that chain souls to the karmic wheel, but the self-seeking motives that inform them. Selfless action, in which the abandonment of selfish desire is practised, will purify the soul so that throughout its earthly existence it may dwell within and upon the waters of the Lake of Peace, reflecting the heavenly light of Brahman, unruffled by the vicissitudes of life and serenely at one with its deeper self.

# the guided visualization

Sit upright, your spine supported if necessary, and ensure that you are comfortable and relaxed. Focus on your heart-centre and breathe gently, easily and slowly. In your mind's eye, let your heart be as a jewel or a crystal into which you are gazing.

You are standing beneath the boughs of a tree in a forest at the breaking of a summer dawn.

A soft cascade of birdsong sounds in the still, cool air, a sweet liquid piping and fluting that seems to be coming from far, far above, as though it is echoing in the grand, solemn space of a temple. The silver-grey light of the early morning has a rapt, enthralled quality, like a beating heart in a lover's expectant breast.

The rays of the rising sun smile suddenly over the waiting forest, and all is transformed. The birdsong becomes a mighty chorus of joy. You listen and watch in rapture as small woodland animals appear in the forest glade before you, intent upon the business of the morning. They are unafraid, showing only curiosity and friendliness as you turn your gaze on them.

With you, they are aware of the presence of Brahma or the Great Spirit and, with you, they offer thanksgiving for the birth of this perfect day.

You are wearing robes that look as though they are composed from the newborn sunlight and the viridian green of springtime leaves. You notice

*You realize that you have been given these shoes to tread softly upon the Earth, to revere and worship her by offering your human love, for she is a loving, living goddess.*

that there are translucent jewels sewn into your clothing, which catch the light in dancing flashes and simultaneously give it out again in shades of their own mystic brilliance.

On your feet are soft shoes made from cloth of gold. The threads in them shine in the sunbeams and, as you begin to walk deeper into the singing forest, it is as if every step you take can heal and bless the Earth with sacred gold from the heart of the sun.

You realize that you have been given these shoes to tread softly upon the Earth, to revere and worship her by offering your human love, for she is a loving, living goddess.

Every step you take is one of jubilance and wonder.

You listen to the birdsong; you taste and smell the clean, fresh, vigorous scents of the woodland; you see the sunlight dancing on the leaves and the forest floor, and the sapphire vault of the skies rolling like a blue carpet of peace over all the world.

It occurs to you that all creation is dancing with the goddess and that it would be good for you to dance too. You dance in a shining glade among the trees, lightly, airily, like a spirit of nature, and it seems to you in your joy that you dance with the scintillating stars and all the turning firmament.

When you have danced to your heart's delight, you rest awhile and then press on deeper and deeper into the forest because you know that some marvel awaits you further on among the trees.

You approach an ancient and majestic tree whose great arching branches create a quiet green sanctuary blessed with fragrant flowers. As you walk around its huge bole, you see that its mighty prehensile roots coil away with serpentine dignity to the shores of a beautiful lake, set like a serene jewel at the great open heart of the forest, its bright waters calm and clear under an enchantment of deepest peace.

You have come to the magical and legendary Lake of Peace.

With reverence, as though you walked on holy ground, you approach the edge of the lake, where reeds stand in contemplation of their graceful reflection in the limpid water. You rest upon the short mossy turf and look out over the lake. The sun is shining, and the cerulean blue of the skies, together with a few clouds, lit with a pure angelic-white radiance, are mirrored in perfect stillness in the fathomless depths.

As you gaze, you begin to notice that the reflections in the water are changing. The image of a wondrous mandala, a sacred pattern inside a revolving wheel, is taking shape within the lake. Its dimensions are those of your own soul. It is a pathfinder to the centre of all things — to the centre of the Great Spirit, the Heart of All, where you have your being and your dwelling

Now you know that the Lake of Peace is indeed the mirror of your eternal self,

and your true reality. Let your heart enter the heart of the mandala reflected in the lake and rest there in deep peace. Now you know that the Lake of Peace is indeed the mirror of your eternal self.

You begin to see that on the other side of the lake the forest has become even more beautiful. All is as before, yet the blessing of the trees, the lake and the sunlit spaces has a greater profundity. The circle of the mandala completes itself, and you are in the heaven worlds.

You are in the enchanted forest of Vrndavana and, between the lofty trees, which are hung with fruits and flowers and fabulous birds that sing with voices of gold and silver, you can see areas of pasturing grass aflame with flowers of every hue, vibrant with unearthly colours that scintillate like dancing lights.

Songbirds like fiery jewels and long-feathered birds of paradise dart and swoop overhead. From the south of the forest, the sweet bell-like notes of many cuckoos sound, and all around there is a burgeoning of deliciously edible vegetation, honeybees and sweet-scented breezes. These refresh and sustain your soul and your spirit, your mind and your body, with a delightful quickening energy that transforms all fatigue, restlessness and sorrow into a hallowed peace and a blessed wellbeing.

You hear the divine notes of Krishna's piping, and see the god and goddess conjoined in their mystical dance between the trees beyond the lake.

---

In wonder you watch, and then you see the form of Krishna, beautiful beyond imagining, advancing towards you from the farther shores.

As he comes, the trees make an avenue for him by bending down their fruitful branches towards his feet. A ring of cuckoos takes flight around his crown, and a higher one of doves encircles him from above. The stags, roes and fauns of the deer folk rush up to meet him with devoted affection, and the honeybees make patterns in the air about him, matching those of the mandala you saw reflected in the depths of the lake. Peacocks dance before him, and the songbirds warble and trill and dive in ecstasy through his aura.

Krishna comes to the very edge of the water and plays his pipe, and your heart is pierced by the loveliness of his essence. You notice a little boat below you, pulled up on to the white sands of the lake's margin.

You rise to your feet, entranced, and walk upon the magical shores of the Lake of Peace. In obedience to the silent command of Krishna, you climb into the boat.

As if charmed, it gently launches itself into the water, and you sail out into the midst of the lake, absorbing its perfect stillness and gentle serenity. Spend some moments gazing out across the calm, hushed waters.

You observe Krishna walking into the waters. He disappears beneath them, but you can still hear the sweet notes of his piping.

He rises in wonderful magnificence right beside your boat, manifesting now as Vishnu, the Preserver, the protector of righteousness and the guardian of all humanity.

Vishnu has taken the form of a fish or a merman, Matsya, and holds up his hands to bless you and to bring you peace.

'Come into the healing waters, my child,' he says to you.

*Your shining self is making the water sparkle with a streaming galaxy of perfect six-pointed stars that connect you to the holy life force ...*

In your body of light you leave the boat and find that you are bathing in the water, as if supported by unseen arms. It washes over you in a baptism of peace, and you see that your shining self is making the water sparkle with a streaming galaxy of perfect six-pointed stars that connect you to the holy life force issuing from Matsya.

You notice that the water of the lake does not prevent you from breathing even when it closes momentarily over your head, but rather enhances it and frees your breath.

'Behold your boat,' says Matsya.

You turn your gaze upon the boat to find that sometimes it seems to hover above the surface of the water, as if it were made of starlight with billowing silver sails, and sometimes it is the simple and humble boat youfound upon the shore, except that strangely it seems to be made of flesh and sinks deeper into the water until half-submerged.

'When you are in your earthly boat,' Matsya reveals, 'and waves of turbulence come to you – waves of emotion, waves of distress, waves of anger and turmoil, waves of intolerance, waves of pain or fear, waves of cynicism and disgust with life and the swamping wave of non-endurance, which follows all these – think of your shining self who is connected to Me at its heart and say these words or give out these thoughts:

'Peace, peace, peace to the violent waves that threaten to overwhelm me. Peace to the troubled brow, peace to the agitated breast, peace to the tormented solar plexus and to the fires below.

'Heart-peace, soul-peace, star-peace, tarashanti, be with me now in the name of the Great Spirit.

'Heart-peace, soul-peace, star-peace, tarashanti, encompass the world and bless the heart of every member of humanity.

'I dwell in silence and stillness within the gentle waters of the Lake of Peace where not a murmur, not a breath, disturbs the great heart of peace where the Spirit dwells.'

Matsya smiles upon you and pronounces his blessing over you: 'Perfect peace, profound peace, the still deeps of peace be forever your dwelling place as you move through the illusions of chaos that try to shatter Peace, peace, peace to you, dear one. Peace of the child within its mother's arms, peace of the child within its father's protection. Peace everlasting, peace ever flowing, peace divine.

the earthly life of the soul. None shall assail you.

'Peace, peace, peace to you, dear one. Peace of the child within its mother's arms, peace of the child within its father's protection. Peace ever-lasting, peace ever flowing, peace divine.'

The lake in the forest, its wonder, its secrets, its enchanted people and the presence of the Great Spirit, begins to recede within you, enfolded into the radiant jewel which is your heart. Come back gently, touch down in the mundane world, carrying these treasures within you.

Return to normal consciousness, seal your centres (crown, brow, throat, heart and solar plexus) with the bright silver cross in a ring of light and make the affirmation inspired by the Lake of Peace.

### affirmation

I bring my mind, my emotions, every thought arising within me, together into the presence of peace. I receive the blessing of peace into my deepest heart. I breathe forth this peace into the heart of the world. I find ways to express peaceful living in my community.

# Meeting the Kontombili

To enrich and deepen your experience of life, let the Kontombili lift
a curtain on its many secrets. This visualization is inspired by the mysteries of African
shamanism, and ushers you into the presence of an exalted people, otherworldly
but real, who bring heart-peace and wise counsel to their human supplicants.

## thoughts from africa

### Lama Khemsar Rinpoche

Everyone of heart on this planet
must respect the existence of every
being. Not only human beings,
but other beings.
(Tibetan Shaman)

### Dagara Prayer

May our ancestors breathe blessing
onto us for our eyes to open,
and our life purpose to become clear.

### Lorraine Mafi-Williams

From out of the spirit world they all came dancing.
The seven spirit brothers and the seven sisters.
The Mi-Mi spirits from space.
Down through the Milky Way they danced
To the earth face below.
They came to dance among the mountains.
In the rivers as they wound their way to the sea.
They danced upon the earth.
They danced upon the rocks.
They danced upon the barks.
And they danced upon the canvas.
They danced in the wind for everlasting life.
They danced the Dreaming alive.
The Mi-Mi spirits from space.

(Aboriginal Shaman)

## the contemplation

Spiritual teachers, seers and esotericists of numerous cultures speak of the god-people who came to Earth in its very beginnings, when humanity was newborn. These god-people came from the stars to instruct humankind, enabling the evolution of beautiful and enlightened civilizations, advanced beyond our wildest dreams, on the continents of Atlantis and Mu.

In time they left, bestowing their legacy in temples and hidden centres, which were guarded by the Elders. These were highly evolved human souls who knew how to use and dispense their magnificent heritage with wisdom, balance and spiritual poise. There were also on the Earth at this time many young souls, who had known very few incarnations. They lived in great joy within these mighty civilizations, which were created by spiritual power to vivify the soul and to harmonize with the natural world.

Unfortunately, the lower nature of these very young souls overcame them, and they stormed the mystery-centres and the temples, forcibly wresting the secrets of the sacred god-power from their rightful keepers. Not being ready to receive such knowledge, they abused it in many ways, swiftly building systems of miraculous but lethal technology. Their evil depredations caused a negative spiritual force to come into being which drew a massive satellite directly into the path of the Earth. All was destroyed, and the sea took back all that had arisen from her. A small scattering of Elders was left to set sail to the farthest shores of the Earth, each bringing their gift of enlightenment to enable humanity to start again.

What we see in the tribes of Africa and other so-called 'primitive' societies are the vestiges of these previous civilizations which were unconscionably more enlightened than the humanity of today. Their rituals and beliefs have seemed to men of 'culture' to be based on vulgar superstition, but this is not so. These people have sacrificed material comfort to keep alive for the sake of their planetary brethren a number of cells of the old knowledge, so that in time we may build again, but this time with perhaps even greater wisdom, humanity and insight, similar civilizations of spiritual power and majesty to those which were ours in the past.

These wisdomkeepers have always protected their knowledge from outsiders, but now, it seems, the young souls who were left on Earth to try to regain their lost paradise have at last attained a degree of preparation and readiness to receive it. Sensing this, and of how disastrous it would be for the future of humanity if their precious cell of knowledge were allowed to die, a young man called Malidoma Patrice Somé, of the West African Dagara people, decided to break the age-old silence and disseminate African wisdom to the world. He wrote an autobiography, entitled *Of Water and the Spirit*, in which he reveals many mysteries concerning the connection of humanity with the spiritual worlds. One of the most direct of these describes his friendship with the Kontombili, a tribe of the inner worlds who are higher up the evolutionary ladder than present-day humanity.

Those Westerners whom he has introduced to the Kontombili speak of a real and moving experience. Many have held the hand of one of these beings for several minutes, the resistance of their narrowly intellectual cultural conditioning melting away in the face of simple reality.

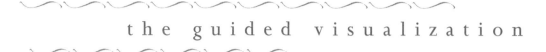

# the guided visualization

Sit quietly and comfortably, clearing your mind by taking several complete breaths. Straighten and relax your spine, using support if necessary. Focus gently on your heart-centre, gradually slow the pace of your breathing, and enter into stillness.

You are moving through a peaceful West African tribal village. The round houses with their conical pointed roofs glow richly golden in the early evening sun. You are aware that their shapes are sacred as you pass them.

Food is being prepared and eaten outdoors, while children and dogs sit at some distance from the domestic fires, a few already asleep. An aura of simplicity and grandeur emanates from the village, the people majestic in their repose. An atmosphere of community spirit and ancient lawfulness pervades the scene, as though the village were built on the site of a temple dedicated to the evocation of a wise and timeless deity.

The village is set upon a wide plain between the foot of a rugged mountain and a great encircling forest. It occurs to you that perhaps the protective temple of the village is the mountain, for you sense that it is holy.

As you come to a cluster of straw granaries bathed in the mellow evening light, a tall, slender man steps out from among them, apparently a member of the tribe, except that there is about him an unearthly beauty of form and feature, and his body throws off a brilliant black incandescence, which you feel as warmth on your skin.

---

You know that he is the Spirit of the Ancestors who forever walks this land, which is the cradle of the human race, and that he will lead you to your greater destiny.

A well-worn path leads down into the village and up the slope of the mountain. The Spirit of the Ancestors beckons to you to follow him along it.

You climb the mountain behind your spirit-guide, enjoying the warm, aromatic air, spiced now with the cooler currents and sharper fragrances of the evening. The way does not seem steep, yet everywhere you look you see grand vistas of the incomparable wilderness of Africa, suffused in sky-pools of fluid golden light.

Your guide leads you to the entrance of a cave, hung with fern fronds and flowering tree creepers. From their depths a huge owl watches you unblinkingly. You feel that the yellow lanterns of its eyes are a signal that you are waited for within. Enter the Sacred Cave with your spirit-guide.

The light is dimly green inside. The cave slopes gently downwards into a beautiful circular hall where once, many thousands of years ago, a whirlpool existed. In the middle of the round hall there is a rock, hewn by ancient waters into the smooth shape of a rustic throne. Facing the throne is a group of stalagmites and stalactites, which lead out of the hall and away down a broad, twisting corridor into the secret heart of the great mountain.

Your guide leads you to the central throne. You move forward to sit in it, but your guide, the Spirit of the Ancestors, signals to you that instead you must kneel before it and lower your forehead on to the rocky dais from which it emerges. You kneel together. You notice that the stone is warm, as though a mighty fire burned in the Earth below the cave floor, like an inner sun. You raise your head almost involuntarily, aware that there is a presence in the hall, centred before you on the throne.

*She is Mother Africa, and also the Great Goddess herself.*

Your eyes fall upon the graceful contours of an immense black goddess. She is seated upon the throne and yet she fills all the hall, the entire mountain and, it seems, even the skies beyond, for you are aware of the twinkling of stars and the turning of planets within the calm vastness of her body. You feel that she is Mother Africa, and also the Great Goddess herself.

With a smile of infinite tenderness she smiles and draws you to her. 'You must recognize and absorb the black Earth energies before your quest can be fulfilled,' she tells you. Her voice is deep and rich as the booming hush of giant waves on some untrodden Pacific shore.

Although you are a minuscule atom within her measurelessness, she takes your hands and looks into your eyes. You suddenly feel that you are a bobbing ball upon the giant plume of a fountain of energy that rises up from the bowels of the Earth and is yet sourced within the heart of the goddess upon her throne. The magical black energies of the Earth rise through you and set you dancing upon their ecstatic peaks.

You feel their power, their goodness, their healing and fecundity, their purity and sanctity, their wonder, their mystery, their beauty – the quintessence of the heart of the Great Mother Goddess. The knowledge comes to you that without these dark energies, so different from the darkness that humankind creates in its foolishness, there could be no springing life upon the Earth and in the cosmos.

As your awareness of the energies recedes, the goddess enters into intangibility, so that her presence still blesses the cave but you can no longer see her seated upon the rocky throne.

The Spirit of the Ancestors leads you forward to another natural outcrop of rock in the approximation of a shrine, which stands before the group of stalagmites and stalactites as they wind away, eerily beautiful, into the fastnesses of the mountain. 'I will leave you here,' he says. 'It has been granted to you to meet with the People of Knowledge.'

Suddenly you are alone in the cave.

You begin to notice a darting, flashing motion beyond the stalagmites, and the appearance of eyes shining in the darkness. Then twelve little human-like creatures, less than 60 cm (2 ft) high, gather before you. They are dark-skinned with West African facial features and long hair, touched with a suggestion of fox-red. Their eyes sparkle and their smile is enigmatic and warm-hearted, dancing with a wise humour.

*It has been granted to you to meet with the People of Knowledge.*

Your communication with them is telepathic. They tell you that they are the Kontombili, that you have come here in quest of the magic of peace, and that they will impart their knowledge of peace to you as a gift.

They lead you to the centre of the cave and indicate to you that you should sit on the throne of rock. You are uncertain, but the Kontombili reassure you that this time it is right for you to do so. 'You are ascending to your Higher Self,' they tell you.

Take your seat upon the throne, and feel the solid caress of the rock as it supports your body. It is easy to sit relaxed and upright in this strange stone chair. Your deeper self, your enlightened self, comes fully into being as you take your first breath upon the chair, and you know that this is because you have found the sacred point of peace within, and that your consciousness was escorted there by the beautiful integrating goddess energies that play eternally around the stone seat.

The Kontombili form a ring around you. Within their circle you feel protected from the emanations of the mundane world. A deep calm descends on you: your irenic self, your spirit, unfurls its wings. In the quietude of this moment, put these questions to the Kontombili, one by one:

'How can I find peace within amidst the pressures and the pace of my everyday life?'

'How can I give peace to all the troubles and anxieties of my psyche?'

'What can I do to promote and nurture peace within my own environment, and within the community in which I live?'

Listen with your inner senses to the answers they give you.

As your time together comes to an end, thank these ancient supernatural people for their gifts of wisdom. Know that you can consult them whenever you take the time to withdraw into the quiet of meditation.

The Kontombili begin to fade into the recesses of the cave. As they take their leave of you, the last to slip away says: 'The state of peace is that which fills you when you walk in the presence of the Divine Spirit. When you are separated from this Great Spirit, then confusion, imbalance, distress, fear, pain and anger can cause war to rage on the inner and the outer planes.'

You contemplate these words as you continue to sit alone on the rocky seat at the heart of the cave. As you do so, you begin to feel a benign presence at your side. It is that of a great master dwelling in the spiritual worlds. He is dressed like a mighty tribal chief in the full regalia of his office, yet his eyes are kindly, and his demeanour, though noble, is gentle.

He guides you safely home with a fatherly air, and imparts some affirmations to you so that you may begin to embrace the philosophy of peace espoused by the Kontombili. Return to normal consciousness, seal your chakras with the bright silver cross in a circle of light, and give forth the affirmation.

### affirmation

I choose peace.
I reject anger, chaos, violence.
I choose peace.
I reject impatience, cruelty, lack of faith.
I choose peace.
I reject fear, pain, condemnation;
all that I reject cannot rise above my
stalwart refusal.
I choose peace.

# The Starlit Canyon

Enter the peace and the wisdom, the mystery and the majesty, of the
Native American spirit-dream: let this visualization guide you to the centre of the
sacred Medicine Wheel, to bring you stillness and calm, and set you on the
beauty-path of the peaceful warrior.

## thoughts from native americans

### Traditional Navajo Song

The mountains,
I become part of it ...
The herbs, the fir tree,
I become part of it ...
The morning mists, the clouds,
The gathering waters,
I become part of it ...
The wilderness, the dewdrops,
the pollen,
I become part of it.

### Tewa Indian Prayer (nineteenth century), USA

Song of the Sky Loom

O our Mother the Earth, O our Father the Sky,
Your children are we, and with tired backs
We bring you the gifts you love.
Then weave for us a garment of brightness;
May the warp be the white light of morning,
May the weft be the red light of evening,
May the fringes be the falling rain,
May the border be the standing rainbow.
So weave for us a garment of brightness,
That we may walk fittingly where birds sing,
That we may walk fittingly where grass is green,
O our Mother the Earth, O our Father the Sky.

## the contemplation

The wisdom and philosophy of the Native Americans is at last beginning to be appreciated in all its mystery, beauty and majesty. It is believed that their civilization is much older than originally thought, and through their legends runs a golden thread of revelation. The spiritual teacher White Eagle speaks of a heritage of folk tales and myths among the tribes, which tell of the coming of the 'feathered gods', who came from afar, bringing a radiance and a salvation. The Native Americans wove these into the fabric of their philosophy and religion.

In her book, *Sun Men of the Americas*, Grace Cooke tells of L. Taylor Hansen's personal encounters with Native Americans, who told him their stories of a saint or prophet, often called Heah-Wah-Sah ('He from Afar Off'), who sailed to their lands. He is described as beautiful, radiant, with fair complexion, fair hair and blue eyes, wearing a white robe with exquisite embroidery of the cross around its edges. He healed the sick, spoke wisdom and brought the dead to life. His symbol was that of the all-seeing eye. L. Taylor Hansen quotes from one of the Elders, an old and venerated Indian, who tells the 'Legend of the Sacred City':

'Tonight I am here to take you walking back through the dawn-star cycles to a time long distant when the land was not as you see it.

'Past the memories of our grandfathers' grandfathers I take you with me to the days of the Healer, and the times of our people's greatness … Coming north from our Capital City, where the Mississippi meets the Missouri, in the longboats of the traders, the Prophet made his journey towards the city we called Sacred …

This city was called Sacred because it was in the centre of the Cross of Waters whence ran the rivers to the Four Oceans. East to the sunrise ran the waters, and northwards to the Sea of Dancing Lights; to the west beyond the Great Divide the waters ran to the Sea of the Sunset, while the Missouri and the Mississippi ran to the Southern Sea, the Sea of the Karibs.

'To this, the City of the Great Cross of Waters, up the river called the Father of Waters, one golden morning came the Healer. The dawn cascaded down upon him as he left the ships of the merchants, painting his hair and beard with beauty and lighting up his lofty features. The streets were petalled with flowers before him as he walked towards the Temple. Greatly beloved now was the Pale God, known as the Lord of Wind and Water. His every move bespoke his kindness, his very touch revealed his divinity and before him bowed down all people.

'Through rows of temple worshippers he moved in quiet solemnity, holding up his hand in blessing, that hand with the strange palm marking, for through it was engraved the cross which he had taken as his symbol.

'There at the temple he abode among us though he often rode away with the merchants or more often walked to distant villages, holding in his hand his great staff, and stopping to speak with all, from the aged to the children.'

L. Taylor Hansen relates other legends of Heah-Wah-Sah: how he came from Venus, instructing his brethren to look to the star as a holy symbol for their prayers and spiritual inspiration; and how he taught his people to resolve their problems by counselling together in peace. The symbol of the Indian peace-pipe is an enduring one. May we ever inhale the spirit, give it out and share it in loving peace.

———

117

# the guided visualization

Begin to draw your breath gently 'through the heart'. Visualize this centre as a sacred crystal of many facets, bearing six points that cast rays of wondrous living brightness in every direction. Dwell quietly at the midpoint of this star-crystal, for it is your true self and its facets are aspects of your soul-temple through which the eternal flame of your spirit shines.

You are drifting in the night sky among the stars. You float very slow-ly, very gently, as if becalmed in an invisible boat. All around you is the quiet darkness and the soft glistening of the stars, twinkling like genie treasure in a vast hidden cave.

One exquisite star shines purer and clearer than all the rest. As you enjoy its bright crystalline radiance, which falls over you with a fairy grace, the certain knowledge comes to you that this celestial body is not a star, but the lovely planet Venus.

*One exquisite star shines purer and clearer than all the rest.*

As this realization breaks like a baptismal wave on your conscious-ness, you gradually begin to spiral downwards with the gentle motion of a dream into a beautiful starlit canyon, which seems to lie directly below the white beams of Venus.

The canyon is deep and silent and dark, although you can see with shadowy clarity by the light of the moon and the stars. Here a Native American warrior awaits you in traditional dress, bearing four shields.

Over his heart he wears a silver six-pointed star with an arrow and heart motif inscribed upon it. You know him to be a Warrior of Peace, charged to challenge and overcome those elements that arise within the sphere of human consciousness, seeking to destroy the harmony and peace of the heart-centred soul.

He leads you to the midpoint of the canyon, where a great medicine wheel has been set out under the stars.

You walk with him to its centre, and he stands with you, tall and majestic, as you both look to the divine South.

He gives you one of his shields. It is red, inscribed with a wave formation and decorated with a crescent moon and wild turkey feathers. Three bands of orange wampum cross its face.

'The moon is the light that shines in the eternal summer of the South. Look through the dancing plant forms and see Black Wolf Spirit. She will lead you to the source of wisdom.'

A garden, strange, wild and beautiful, seems to have grown up in the place of the South. You see a spectral black wolf, and allow your spirit to follow its lead deep into the garden wilderness.

The garden is dancing, the plant forms lovely and ethereal. They sing with sweet chanting voices and emit strains of music. They clear suddenly under the crescent moon, and you come to a lagoon of pure water.

Under the moon, a mysterious figure repeatedly dives and re-emerges from the water, coming to rest on a crystal rock. As you draw nearer you see that she is a woman bearing the form of a mouse. Both shapes manifest in vivid coexistence.

'Who comes here to seek Diving Mouse Woman?' she asks.

Under the moon, a mysterious figure repeatedly dives and re-emerges from the water, coming to rest on a crystal rock.

Give her your name by saying it out loud.

You look into the eyes of Diving Mouse Woman, and see there the trust and innocence of a child. You understand that these qualities cannot be exposed recklessly and thoughtlessly to the harshness of the outside world but must be protected within the wisdom and divine will of the spirit.

As you comprehend this truth, you see also that you must be constantly vigilant to protect the child within you and all the children of the world, for from the eyes of Diving Mouse Woman there shines not only the sweetness of the infant but also the love and mighty care of Divine Mother. Diving Mouse Woman escorts you back to your past, and allows you to comfort and nurture the child within your own nature.

Diving Mouse Woman begins to leap in and out of the water again, and this time you note her mouselike qualities, which surprise you with their scope and unexpectedness. You see that the mouse is endlessly resourceful, nimble and alert. Your human wits are not quick enough to follow its every movement. The mouse is playful, curious, eager; it is meticulous and methodical; it is bold and daring; it pushes boundaries; it is cheeky. It has a celerity of movement and decision that is breathtaking and a ferocity of will that can often outface human determination. It has an unquenchable zest for life. The only weakness of the mouse is fear, which can make it panic blindly.

You see that Diving Mouse Woman is contained within the feeling body, the emotional body of your soul. You realize that this precious lagoon must be cherished and protected by the wise heart-light of your spirit, for it leaps with joyful life and feeds your whole consciousness.

Black Wolf Spirit returns and leads you back to the centre of the medicine wheel. Before you step over the threshold, your Native American warrior guide says to you: 'Open your being to the lessons of this sacred orientation, and to all the beauty, power and revelations that come to your heart from the South.'

You obey his exhortation and see an enchanted city in the South called Finias. Its sign is a spear, a fiery point that is destined to penetrate the heart so that it may wake and live, slaying all the dross of the being. It says: 'Remove the Veil of Fear!'

You step over the threshold of the medicine wheel, and turn with your guide to the magical West.

You find that the first shield has blended with your soul and is no longer manifest. Black Wolf Spirit hands you the second shield. It is decorated with osprey feathers, and inscribed with the symbol of a mountain with a single flowering tree growing from it. It is black with touches of gold, and crystals have been sewn into its deer hide. It bears two black bands.

'Earthshine and the ancient signs of the zodiac light the fruitful autumn of the West,' says your guide. 'Look upon the Place of Stones and follow Darting Bird Spirit to your destination.'

Darting Bird Spirit comes swooping into your field of vision, and you climb after her into the Place of Stones. Great boulders surround you, although they glimmer with half-hidden precious gems. All around you the

countryside bears the soft dun shades and fiery colours of autumn, and in the early morning sky a perfect, conical ring of pearly radiance sits like a crown upon heaven's dome. You know that it is the beautiful phenomenon of the Zodiacal Light.

Darting Bird Spirit leads you to a deep cave. You pass within. A great, shadowy bear is dancing in the mellow underworld dusk. You feel the dark, secret, potent and healing energies of the Earth. You speak your name out loud to the bear.

The bear speaks: 'Dance with me, human soul, for I am your sister. I am Dreaming Bear.'

You dance with your sister, Dreaming Bear, and, as you dance, you hear the beat of drums and the keening, exhilarating throb of Native American victory songs. Your two dancing figures throw impossibly huge shadows on the great walls of the cave. Bizarrely, the shadow of Dreaming Bear is no greater than your own.

As you dance, you sense that Dreaming Bear is indeed a great dreamer, for she spends almost half the year in hibernation, dreaming the Great Dream and studying magical inner wisdom. You become aware of her power, of her massive stored energies. She is in truth a spirit of the sacred Earth.

You consider the splitting of the atom and the untold power reserves held in the physical atoms of Mother Earth. You think of her wild stone heart, not cold and hard but loving, emanating warm and nurturing energy, like the ineffable beauty of her crystal self, of which half her body consists. And yet humans experience the Earth-state as inertia, powerlessness.

You think of your own physical body, your revered temple, the holy receptacle for divine spirit and its manifestation. You consider the sanctity of ancient artefacts, and how the ancient cycles must return, for nothing dies; rather it is transformed as it passes through the body of the great Earth Mother. You feel how important it is to express Mother Earth's goodness and wholesomeness, her vitality and her beautiful energies by adhering to uncontaminated, natural foods, and of how these give good mental and emotional as well as physical health, keeping you firmly anchored in the rich, life-giving soil of the Eternal Now.

As Darting Bird Spirit returns and you take your leave of Dreaming

Bear, you sense that the mysteries of the Earth are far greater and deeper and more sublime than humanity has ever conceived. You find yourself back at the threshold again, ready to re-enter the heart of the medicine wheel.

Your guide says to you: 'Open your being to this magical orientation, and to all the beauty, power and revelations that have come to your heart from the West.'

You see the enchanted city of Murias twinkling in the mystery of the declining West. Its sign is a miraculous hollow filled with water and fading light, the essence of earthshine which so mysteriously and dimly lights the heavens. It is the emanation of the veiled, inscrutable Earth Mother. It says: 'Remove the Veil of Shame!'

You step back into the middle of the medicine wheel, and your guide passes to you the third shield. Once again, your hands are empty to receive it, because the shields of the South and the West have secreted themselves within your soul.

The shield of the East has a golden hue. It seems to flow with golden hair. It is decorated with golden eagle feathers and emblazoned with suns and spirit-forms in fountains of fire. It bears one yellow band upon which a single eye is engraved.

'Grandfather Sun lights the vernal skies of the Bright Land,' says your guide. 'Let Golden Warrior Woman lead the way, for your path penetrates the mysteries of the human heart.' Beautiful, radiant, gracious and kindly,

*Grandfather Sun lights the vernal skies of the Bright Land.*

Golden Warrior Woman lifts you into the Bright Land on the currents of her sweet breath. She carries you to a mountain top. There, wheeling above you in the blue, is a great golden eagle.

'Who is it that comes seeking Grandfather Eagle?' he cries. You speak your name aloud and he drops to a rock in line with your brow-centre, the topmost peak of the mountain. He holds you in his vision with his sharp unblinking eye. 'You'll do,' he says, and launches suddenly into the air, giving three terrible shrieks.

They seem to resound in you and make you stagger back. When you regain your balance, the world has changed. You are in a sphere of inconceivably brilliant radiance. Your mind, your vision, your heart has never comprehended the possibility of such ecstasy, such glory, pulsing forth, giving forth, self-perpetuating, self-replenishing.

Beyond the disc, its source and its centre, is the perfect shape of a six-pointed star, calm as a vision of paradise.

'You are in the heart of the sun,' says Grandfather Eagle. 'Dear one, do you not know that this is your own essence? How can you doubt yourself or your power to overcome, when this is your true home?'

You listen to Grandfather Eagle's words, and you feel a magnificent brotherhood, sisterhood, with every member of humanity and with all life. You see it go from you like a great ray of light, a beam of clarifying power. You see it cleansing heavy sullied clouds until they are silver cascades of laughing, endless light.

Grandfather Eagle bobs with joy. 'Those are the clouds of misery and weariness that creep into the vision of those on Earth,' he explains. 'Such clouds cannot resist the sun. The weakness of the East in human understanding is their way of perceiving death and decay. Humans do not see that it is but a transformation and a letting-go. They think it is a destination! The great sun laughs and dances at such folly! Now I will take you to the Place of Vision, so that you may be sure never to share in such blindness.'

A wheel of light rotates, and you are standing before a great pine tree. Beyond is a garden where the sun-spirits dance. It is of such pulchritude that you cannot see beyond the pine tree; you only dimly know what is there in your deepest being.

The pine tree deposits a small, bright golden cone into your palm. Grandfather Eagle instructs you to press it to your brow-centre.

'Now you are awakened,' he says. 'The gift from the sacred pine tree will enable you to see with the vision of your heart. Awaken the golden pine cone by breathing quietly, by going to your heart-centre. Then your true eye will open, the all-seeing eye of your god-self, your gift from the tree. Many call it the-mind-in-the-heart.'

Grandfather Eagle again rotates a wheel of light. You feel a rush of ether and you are back on the mountain top. There he teaches you how the

*Grandfather Eagle teaches you that his kind are messengers from the spirit, and that the spirit is the heart of everlasting love.*

eagle can look unflinchingly into the heart of the sun; how it soars above all lower things and overcomes their gravity pull, so that its nobility is never dishonoured; and how it takes the straight path into the grand heights, without distraction or delay, so that its vision is unconfined and all-embracing.

Grandfather Eagle teaches you that his kind are messengers from the spirit, and that the spirit is the heart of everlasting love.

Golden Warrior Woman comes to return you to your Native American guide. She gently wafts you on her fragrant currents of breath to the threshold of the eastern quarter of the medicine wheel.

Your guide addresses you: 'Open your being to the lessons of this mystical orientation, and to all the beauty, power and revelations that come to your heart from the East.'

You see the magical city of Gorias glittering in the rising sun, and a pure sword of flashing light which is its sign. You know that it is the sword of the spirit, which must be wielded by every member of humanity, and that it points the way to humanity's future, saying, 'Remove the Veil of Self-Doubt!'

You step over the threshold and, with your guide beside you, you turn at last to the sacred North. He gives you the last shield.

It is white, like a white sun. It is hung with white feathers, and decorated in wampum with the motifs of birds, animals and stars. Four golden bands cross its face.

---

'The way of the North is lit by the mystery of the stars in its rapt Winter Dream. Star Elk Spirit will show you the way.'

A male elk appears before you, bearing magnificent antlers. You touch his nose hesitantly and he nuzzles your hand. Then he turns his great shoulders and walks into a shining mist.

You follow him, penetrating the shimmering mist, which dances around you in spears of rose, white, blue and green that glow with a deep glassy luminescence, like mirrored pools of light.

As you move further into these dancing, billowing lights, you begin to perceive many different animal shapes all around you. Some are well known to you, others are the great animals of the grassy plains, and still others are completely unfamiliar, except that you recognize a fabulous or a mythical beast now and again.

You come to a ring of glimmering white rocks that seems suspended in the night sky. Nevertheless, there is a world here: the landscape is covered in pure white snow.

The mists part and you see clearly that the ring of stones is peopled by tall and beautiful men and women, mighty of stature and dressed in ethereal, flowing clothes similar in some respects to the ceremonial dress of the Native American.

Star Elk Spirit speaks. 'These are the Star People. This sphere of the air is their Lodge. They will invoke White Buffalo Woman for you. You are indeed honoured.'

The ceremony begins, flowing and pulsing in sweet and superb rhythm and song, moving in exhilarating cycles until a great white buffalo appears on the far horizon. It seems to descend from a group of stars softly glimmering with muted fire, a constellation you know to be the Pleiades, the Seven Sisters. It half-rears on the skyline and then gallops towards you with a smooth, undulating motion.

As the buffalo draws closer, you see that it is a woman who approaches you, a woman of miraculous beauty and grace, who bears within her form the presence of a great white buffalo. She is clothed in milk-white buffalo skins of fathomless purity. Around her flows an aura of pearly essence and the white peace of newly fallen snow.

'Who is it that summons White Buffalo Woman?' she asks you, and you speak aloud your name.

A deep stillness follows. In your spirit-body you kneel at the feet of White Buffalo Woman, for you see that here is Divine Mother, who in her perfect love for her human child gives of herself utterly and entirely.

*In your spirit-body you kneel at the feet of White Buffalo Woman*

For every part of the buffalo gave life to her children of the plains: she gave them food, clothes, materials for constructing their tipis and bone tools to facilitate their everyday lives. Even the teeth of the buffalo gave them shamanic charms and protection. Behind the roving buffalo herds stood

White Buffalo Woman, cherished spirit-mother to her people, endlessly bestowing her grace, her gifts, her essence.

Held within the tender white radiance of this great being, you realize deep within yourself that every human soul must learn to emulate her purity, her loving service, to give unstintingly of itself, holding nothing back, asking nothing in return, lifting human giving above barter and control. And you see also that receiving White Buffalo Woman's gifts without appreciation and humility gives rise to an arrogant certainty, which is the weakness of the North for the human soul. You see that certainty must only be experienced and expressed concerning principles, never details.

Deeply you contemplate these things, deeply you withdraw into the peace of your heart-centre to fathom the meaning and the beauty of these profound truths, for you see that meaning is beauty, and beauty is meaning.

The presence of White Buffalo Woman touches your heart and makes you long to honour your own Beauty Path, the flight path of your spirit. Star Elk Spirit tosses his head and paws the ground, ready to escort you safely

back to the centre of the medicine wheel. White Buffalo Woman has taken her path to the stars and has returned to the bright Pleiades.

You give thanks to the graceful Star People, recognizing that they are angels. As you follow Star Elk Spirit back through the dancing, leaping, coloured mists, you realize that they are the northern lights and that you have penetrated their secret citadel.

You reach the threshold of the northern quarter of the medicine wheel. Your guide awaits. He says to you: 'Open your being to the lessons of this sacred orientation, and to all the beauty, power and revelations that come to your heart from the North.'

You see the fabled city of the spirit of the North played over by a deeply dreaming occult light, the visionary light of the Ancient of Days. It is Falias, and its sign is the stone of the transformation which is death, crowned by pale, flickering fire. It says: 'Banish the Veil of Self-Will, for it is rooted in arrogance, narrowness and partial sight! Flow with Divine Will and you shall spread peace and beauty across the world.'

You cross the threshold to your guide. He tells you: 'Now you must accept the fifth shield.'

Overhead, the peaceful stars and a new crescent moonshine down into the silent, still, shadowed canyon. You stand at the centre of the medicine wheel with your guide.

As if a mist has fallen away from your eyes, you see that you are standing in a glen of precious stones. Its beauty and its peace are measureless. 'This is the fifth city,' says your guide. 'It is the consecrated wedding place of the soul and the spirit, where they conjoin and become as one.

Each gem is a solid structure of knowledge and experience that you have used to capture and contain the light of your soul, the wisdom of the stars. These structures too must pass away, so that only the living light remains – dynamic, free and transformational.'

Looking up, you gaze at Venus, shining in the night sky. Your perception shifts and it is as if you are suddenly looking up at a city of angels within the heart of the bright planet. As you watch, you perceive that the glen of precious stones magically becomes one with this angelic city, as though there is an ascension and a descent and an interpenetration.

You see that your guide is kneeling, and you kneel beside him. Before you stands the white-robed figure of a man with shining eyes, bearing the sign of the medicine wheel, the cross within the circle.

*Before you stands the white-robed figure of a man with shining eyes, bearing the sign of the medicine wheel, the cross within the circle.*

With great gentleness and love, he gives you your fifth shield. You see that it is made of light. It is decorated with the cross within the circle, the all-seeing eye, and a ring of hands. All its symbols are lit by stars, for this shield seems to contain the very galaxy itself.

'Make of your soul a song to the Great Spirit,' the white-robed man says. 'Pray to the winds; the Great Spirit will hear you. Pray to the galaxy, set your light-body walking on the Milky Way; the Great Spirit will bless you. Let the sun and the moon guide you, and let your spirit dwell often upon the beauty and mystery of Venus, for she has much to teach the stumbling children of Earth. But, above all, turn again and again to the star that resides in your heart, for that is the Great Spirit's source. Do these things and you shall know peace.'

He blesses both you and your guide before disappearing as the fifth city recedes into mystery. You find yourself standing at the centre of the simple medicine wheel. 'We have met with Heah-Wah-Sah, the Healer, Lord of Wind and Water, the holy Prophet-God of the Native American Tribes,' says your guide. 'We have met with He Who Will Come Again.'

As day breaks in the cool pure air of the canyon and Venus shines silver below the brilliant circle of the early morning sun, a deep knowledge is conveyed to you that humanity is standing on the brink of a new dawn that will bring deep and abiding peace to all the nations of the world, from North to South, from East to West.

Feel the vision comforting, healing and inspiring every level of your being, enabling you take up your life anew as a Warrior of Peace, guided always by the wise and peacemaking warrior who walks eternally by your side.

Gently return to normal waking consciousness, seal your centres (crown, brow, throat, heart, solar plexus) with the bright silver cross in a circle of light, and earth yourself if necessary. Now make the affirmation of the Warrior of Peace.

### affirmation

I walk my beauty-path in peace.
Peace flows to me from the stars.
I am a Warrior of Peace.

# The Garden of Delights

Let the contemplation and visualization on the following pages,
inspired by the words of the Sufi mystic Rumi and the wisdom of the Islamic faith,
bring you peace in everyday life. When in need of calm and support,
find comfort in these words.

## thoughts from islam

### The Prophet Mohammed

#### A Muslim Prayer

O Allah!
You are the giver of Peace;
from You comes Peace;
Blessed are You
O Possessor of Majesty
and Honour.

### Raficq Abdulla

#### Seeking the Beloved

Whirl and rejoice, find the ruby of your heart
Through circling degrees, your body becoming
A planet of the soul embedded in still serenity.
You are your arching senses sending energy
To the centre of the dance: the Beloved calls out
To himself rising like Leviathan rejoicing.
Wars are fought here in your dancing blood
Chamber convulsed with joy. It looks upon God
From the famine of its lowly state with longing sighs.
Angels pierce you in your turning with the cool
Needles of their eyes, you are wounded with
Their peace, you whirl and rejoice, happily drowning
In that enchantment where no body may enter,
No sun nor moon, as the dancer brings forth the dance.

## the contemplation

This meditation is inspired by the Islamic religious tradition. The Prophet Mohammed spoke of the 'Heavenly Garden' in the Koran:

'And Allah summoneth to the abode of peace, and leadeth whom He will to a straight path. For those who do good is the best (reward) and more (thereto). Neither dust nor ignominy come near their faces. Such are the rightful owners of the Garden; they will abide therein.'

Sufism is its mystical sect, in which devotees find union with Allah in the whirling dervishes, instituted by the famous poet, thinker and Sufi scholar Jalal Al-Din Rumi, who was born in present-day Afghanistan in the thirteenth century. This circling dance, when undertaken in a spirit of devotion, induces a change of consciousness in which visionary meditations are experienced.

In this way, another Sufi master and poet, Muhyiddin Ibn Arabi, was given revelations of the Heavenly Garden. The Sufi master described this Garden as the 'Earth of True Reality':

'In that Earth there are gardens, paradises, animals, minerals … Everything that is to be found on that Earth, absolutely everything, is alive and speaks, has a life analogous to that of every living being endowed with thought and speech. Endowed with thought and speech, the beings there correspond to what they are here below, with the difference that, in that celestial Earth, things are permanent, imperishable, unchangeable; their universe does not die.'

In Jannah, the Garden of Paradise, the Beloved appears in the lovely aspect of As-Salam, the Lord of Peace and the Giver of Peace. The word 'Islam' itself is derived from 'salam', meaning 'peace'.

The Prophet said to all those who recognized the Divine Presence in their hearts: 'You will not enter the Garden of Paradise until you believe; and you shall not believe until you love one another. Shall I guide you to a thing that when you practise it will cause you to love one another? Spread as-Salam [the peace of God] among yourselves.'

The Garden of Paradise is an expression of 'Dar as-Salam', the everlasting 'Home of Peace'. We can enter it via our spiritual selves whilst still here on Earth, using meditation to open a door into the Garden. And perhaps, on returning, we can seek to spread as-Salam, so that the mundane Earth may be brought into greater attunement with the 'Earth of True Reality'.

# the guided visualization

Sit comfortably, spine upright, supported if necessary, and breathe quietly and easily, a little more deeply than usual.

Begin to imagine that you are walking peacefully upon a high plateau. The wind blows softly through the whispering grasses and stirs your hair playfully. You look out on the beautiful, wild mountainous region all around, gazing quietly at the dreaming blue haze in the distance. You have come here to be at peace and to allow your soul to run free.

*You have come here to be at peace and to allow your soul to run free.*

There is a hush over the land, made deeper by the sweet warbling song of a lonely mountain bird. Evening is drawing near, and the sunlight has taken on a rich, mellow brightness. Soon a pale green, amethyst and heavenly blue luminous dusk gathers, creating a fairy world of muted light shining in the bosom of the clouds floating above the shadowed peaks.

In that magical twilight, shining bright trails of stars appear and dance with a gentle silver fire. It is as if a smiling hallowed spirit were offering a welcoming hand to your human soul, bidding it follow that mystical trail and ascend to dimensions of mystery and wonder where the heart laughs in bliss.

Contemplating the scene, your soul rises within you and scintillates in a flame of joy, giving thanks for the magic of the evening. In this heightened state, in which hordes of shining eyes seem to keep on opening within you, you suddenly see what appears to be a wall. It stretches on and on across the land and into space. It is all around you, not imprisoning you or barring your way, but rather hiding, protecting, obscuring what lies beyond.

As you gaze at the wall, so impregnable and yet misty, glimmering and ever-changing like the imponderable stars, a miracle happens. A great angel, golden and glorious as the rising sun, takes form before your eyes. He spans the horizon, and the ethereal wall begins and ends within his aureole of perfect golden light.

An interior voice says: 'Behold the Archangel Michael,' and with awe and reverence you bathe in the radiance of this magnificent being.

As you absorb his brilliant light, your own wings take shape and spread behind you. Though you remain standing where you are, you feel your soul take flight and soar into the heaven worlds. The Archangel Michael opens his arms to receive you, and you realize that his form has become that of a gateway, mighty, arched and pillared. It is open to you. Wondering, you walk forward as into the rays of a dazzling star.

There is a garden here beyond the walls. And yet, when you turn to look back, there are no walls: they have dissolved into the gentle sunshine, and everywhere there are the playing golden rays of Michael, of the sun, and of some ineffable mystery of Being above these.

---

You turn again to the garden, eager to explore. This is the Garden of Delights, and everywhere you look there are wonders.

You see that not only are the golden rays playing all over the garden, but that the most delicate rainbow colours are everywhere present like subtle laughing flames. There are other colours too, colours you have never seen on Earth, which speak to and sound notes within your soul so that it emanates a strange and lovely music. Stand awhile, bathing in these glorious, rejoicing colours as they caress you with their heart-awakening voices.

Your feet sink into sun-warmed grass, emerald and cool in its depths. These lawns are starred with tiny, jewel-coloured flowers, which cluster around your toes. They call to you with bell-like voices to follow the path they make. You set your feet on the path and, as you take your first steps, you *Your feet sink into sun-warmed grass, emerald and cool in its depths.* can hear every vibrant grass blade whispering songs of praise into the gently sighing wind, which breathes lightly, revivifying your own breath.

You walk across the glowing green lawns towards a rose garden that is laid out in a sacred spiral along curving paths of clear crystal. Each rose bush reaches almost your own height, and is burgeoning with a glorious pageant of roses, which look as though they spilled from the heart of an angel. Foaming billows of lush rose-heads surge and flow on each side, springing into the air in a burst of colour and an ecstasy of perfume, forcing your senses to expand and grow to encompass their reality.

Walk amongst the roses to the very centre of the spiral.

*Take the path to your heart.*

There, among the tumbling, intoxicating roses, stands a white boulder. It speaks to you, and its voice is like bee-song, vibrating on many levels:

'Come to the centre, child of Earth. Take the path to your heart.'

You feel a surge of love for this being of stone and you pass into what seems to be its arms. You enter a moment of blazing white light. Beyond it stretches another garden, although you know that it is simply a deeper dimension of the same garden.

This garden is like the last, only wilder and sweeter airs blow about it. Within its precincts there are little sunlit woods, a clear tranquil lake and wild turf crowded with tiny, star-like flowers of a thousand vivid hues. It rolls away like a gentle wave, creating miniature hills and dells in its swell.

You stand awhile to watch and listen as birds and beasts of great beauty come and go, without timidity or aggression. They are a part of the peace, givers and receivers of the Divine Love that breathes everywhere as a holy radiance, a holy fragrance, a mysterious omnipotence. It dances upon the waters of the lake on the wind so the ripples shake and laugh with joy.

As you listen, you become aware that the trees are singing hymns of great and ancient beauty. You are drawn into their music, absorbing their might, their grandeur, their nobility of spirit. Above you in the vast, deep-hearted ocean of cerulean blue skies, shining white clouds build mystic temples of blissful purity. 'Human soul, hear what we say! The time will come when these temples that we are showing you will appear everywhere on your

Earth! And when those days are with you, humankind shall know that all the Earth is a Most Holy Temple!'

You realize that the clouds have spoken to you. In wonder, you contemplate that in the Garden of Delights the stones speak, the trees sing, the clouds prophesy, and the water and the winds dance and laugh. All share in a sublime consciousness that magically dwells at the centre of your heart.

Recognizing this great truth, your spirits become even more light and airy, and you are filled with a childlike joy. In this new innocence, you climb the little, flower-strewn hill that lies before you.

You soon reach the top, from which you look down on a sight that is the essence of paradise. Spreading before you is a precious and sacred valley. It gives you its name. It is the Many-coloured Valley, and it is a dale of abundant, supernaturally beautiful summer flowers, each radiating its own exquisite hue as if lit by an inner luminescence.

Springs rise everywhere, making natural fountains of crystal purity. Its perfume and its rapturous colours, its ten thousand jubilant flower forms fill you with an ecstasy of beauty and mystery. As a child you run down into the valley, as though some divine soul of motherhood waited there to receive you, and you feel the welcoming caress of the soft, heavenly scented petals.

And now you feel the Holy Presence of someone, some Being of inconceivable magnitude, in the heart of which you live and move and have your being. It is the Lord of the Garden, the Beloved!

You feel the Holy Presence of someone, some Being of inconceivable magnitude.

You kneel at the feet of this Great Spirit, this inscrutable Presence, and you are filled with a deep, deep peace. Heavenly peace fills the craters of your need. Your body melts away in peace.

*... you are filled with a deep, deep peace.*

Your heart rests in the vast ocean of peace, which is the Heart of the Beloved. Your mind is released from its restless tides and becomes as serene as a soundless, motionless lake, reflecting the sublime peace of the Beloved. Your emotional self becomes a white dove of peace. Your soul is transfigured into a shining angel of peace by the healing balm that is the breath of the Beloved. All is peace, and the Beloved is All.

You are aware that the Beloved has transported you to a spiritual mountain top. And yet, magically, miraculously, you are still in the arms of the valley of flowers. You are free upon the glorious mountain top and yet simultaneously cradled protectively within the sacred valley.

The flowers of the valley form a single rose upon the radiant mountain top. The rose is aflame with the light of the Beloved. In peace you enter its heart, its temple. Step within, and know that the Lord of the Garden and the Valley Spirit will guide you safely home, and dwell within you always.

Touch down gently, become aware of the familiar things around you, and seal your centres. Now make the affirmation of the Garden of Delights meditation.

### affirmation

The peace of the Beloved fills my heart.
I am eternally replenished from the source of peace.
I give this unending peace to everyone I meet.
I give this ever-replenished peace to all the world.

# The Candle of Vision

When life appears to lose all its magic and grace, and only its harsh vibrations and jarring experiences seem to be real, turn to the symbol of the Candle of Vision to unlock your imagination. Let this guided visualization, inspired by the seers, mystics and spiritual teachers of our time and by the Star of the Aquarian Age, lead you to the creative point of peace within.

## thoughts from the new faith

### White Eagle: The Lightbringer

The six-pointed star is the most beautiful symbol of the perfectly balanced soul, the soul whose head is in the heavens, whose faculties are quickened to receive the light from above, and whose feet are firmly planted upon the road of earth, which the soul traverses with one object in view – to find and give true happiness of the spirit.

Whichever way you turn it and whichever way you use it, it remains the same: perfectly balanced, a focal point (if held with love, concentration and devotion) to attract the angelic hosts from the spiritual spheres who work ceaselessly for the power of the Spirit to manifest on earth. Where the star shines by the will and through the love of earthly men and women, the effect over chaos and disorder, war, and all the evils in the world can be truly magical.

### White Eagle: The Book of Starlight

Above you is a Star of infinite light, beauty, power and love. From this star the light is pouring down upon you. Attune yourself to this central point of power. It is your life. The Star, which is a symbol of the highest life, is within your heart as well as blazing in the heavens. You are all small stars: you are building the Star of life within your own soul. As you learn to become powerful under the Star, you radiate this peace into the outer world.

### Augustine of Hippo Regius

Late have I loved Thee O Beauty
ever ancient and ever new!

# the contemplation

Many people today are looking forward with hope and faith to the establishment of a new worldwide religion that will be based on individual awareness and growth towards the light of the spirit; a free religion whose church will be the sanctuary of the heart. Fed by the ancient springs of the deeper truths in all religions, this new faith will contain no dogma, no creed except the individual perception of the guidance of the spirit towards creating a happy, kindly, just community on planet Earth that will provide for the fullest expression of the light-channelling soul.

Once we begin to unfold our spiritual perception, we will find many sources to guide and instruct us; and each culture will be inspired in its creative building at the inner and outer level by its 'ancestors', those who have gone before and now dwell in a world of light.

Above all will shine the ineffable radiance of the god-goddess and its issuing Divine Child, which bears its light to humanity by showing us the way home. This may be through the figure of Jesus, Buddha or Krishna; it may be through those who have gone before whom we call saints or ancestors, or even the highly advanced god-men and god-women who preceded our Earth; it may be through the magical tribes dwelling within the finer essence of matter known to African shamanism; it may be through the Tree of Life revealed by Judaism, or the whirling path and the straight path to the Islamic garden of unity and light; or it may be through the mystical wind blowing like a whispering breath through the ascending way of Shin-to and Lao-tzu.

The symbol of the New Age of Aquarius is the Star – a deeply magical and powerful symbol of the spirit. It is formed from two equilateral triangles which meet and interpenetrate to express the perfect shape of the six-pointed star. This form is understood by esotericists to stand behind the Sun's disc and its emanations, and can perhaps be thought of as the Sun's divine chakra, the mystical point at which the inconceivable power and glory of the Great Spirit connects with the physical Sun and pours forth its supernal rays of creation, that spiritual force within matter, the spiritual light within physical light.

Each human heart contains the metaphysical presence of a star. Using the gentle rhythm of the breath and the power of inner vision, we can locate this star and send out its light to heal ourselves and loved ones (including animals) who are in distress or danger, and to bring blessing and peace to all the world.

The physical and spiritual forces are especially in alignment on the point of the magical hours of three, six, nine and twelve throughout the day and night. We might think of each as an in-breath for the physical sphere.

On the in-breath, we receive the light of the star. Just think of it blazing in the heavens and in your own heart. Its light is an expression of perfect love, perfect peace, perfect integration or healing. On the out-breath, we give out the light. Give it out to your workplace, your office, your classroom, your home, your garden. Give it out to the world.

If you do this regularly, on a daily basis if possible, you will have no need of proof or faith that the star is real and working. The evidence will be all around you, and you will be numbered among the blessed peacemakers of the world.

# the guided visualization

Sit in a comfortable and relaxed position, spine straight, supported if necessary. Focus your awareness at your heart-centre and softly draw the breath 'through the heart', breathing a little more slowly and deeply than usual.

Light a white candle or create a lucid image of a lighted candle. With gentle concentration, sit and watch your candle for a while. It is the Candle of Vision, and in your higher awareness you know that its unearthly counterpart burns brightly and unquenchably. You know, too, that it is as if the candle with its glowing flame were a mirror, for in your heart-centre your eternal self coruscates like a spearhead of light and can never be extinguished.

Focus now on that flame in your heart, ever giving forth a soft, holy radiance that would light up all your being and all your life if you allowed it to do so. It is the light of peace, emanating from a great cosmic heart of love.

Keep that still flame in your mind's eye as you go deeper into the inner worlds, even though other visions rise and unfold before you.

You are standing at the margin of a mountainside woodland. Little mists white as virgin snow curl and weave upon its floor, and bracing and vigorous airs blow about it and make the trees rustle softly and strangely, with an almost articulate voice. It is sunrise, early in the spring, and the morning wears the garments of winter but dances with the spirit of summer in all her delight and promise.

The mountain breeze is so clean, cool and life-giving that you feel that you are at the very edge of the world, watching the first dawn break. The colours in the sky are a great spreading mystery of crimson brilliant as the flashing of a jewel, of drifting rose, sweet gold and muted celandine, sparkling white-silver and soft angel blue. There is magic in this sunrise, and, as if to verify your recognition of it, a voice calls your name from the depths of the sunny wood.

You hardly know if the voice is real or imaginary, but you are moved to respond to it anyway by a deep soul-impulse. You walk into the flowering woods. As sweet aromas arise from the bracken and the fresh, wholesome Earth, you become aware of other perfumes, flower scents, including the delicate incense of bluebells, creating enchanted pools below the trees.

They give forth a wild fragrance, the essence of carefree childhood happiness, and from their midst a bird of beautiful song flies up and perches

*great cosmic heart of love.*

on a branch just above your head, pouring out its rapture to the morning in a mellifluent flood of bell-like, crystal notes. It is a woodlark and, as you engage with his bright eye, you realize that he is leading you to some secret, lovely place, deep in the magical woodland.

As you pass a huge, majestic oak wound around with ivy, you enter a wide glade that, breathtakingly, is a sequestered garden set like a mystic jewel in the heart of the wood. Birds of many colours flit from branch to branch, and everywhere you look, full of wonder, burgeoning flowers of every dream-engendered hue climb, twine and pour from bushes or glow among the grass like a meeting of rivers from the heart of paradise.

Entranced, you gaze around at the radiant inner forms of the trees and the flowers, at the soft emerald grass at your feet, and at the rainbow wealth of the flowers.

You inhale their perfume and consider their perfection of form. Every leaf, every blade, every petal shares the sublime consciousness of the Great Spirit, of the dancing goddess. And now you, the pilgrim soul, are looking into the mystical heart of the garden with eyes of the spirit.

Where is the mystical heart of the garden? You know where it lies because the point of consciousness where it dwells is given to you, as if by the whisper of the goddess, as if on the breath of angels.

Look deep, deep into this mystical heart and begin to see a soul-form taking shape. It is the bright-white, lightly tripping unicorn, mighty and ancient of spirit, kindly and gentle of demeanour, of measureless grace and beauty, radiating a hallowed peace. Your deeper self is about to receive the shining vision of the unicorn into its heart.

> Look deep, deep into this mystical heart
> and begin to see a soul-form taking shape.

You see its horn, gleaming golden-white, its white flanks shining with a pure radiance, its fathomless eyes alight with a strange glory that pierces your heart with a shaft of Divine Love. The unicorn recognizes you, knows you! It was the voice of the unicorn that called to you so that you responded to its bidding and came in search of the miracle of its being. Bathe in the wonder and the gladness and the deep heart-peace of this moment.

Begin to call out in answer to the unicorn. Let it be a call from your soul to your spirit. You do not need to use words; simply allow this soul-call to rise up and to go forth from your heart.

Alerted, the unicorn raises its noble head. Its rippling white mane moves in the winds of the spirit. Responding, its body poised in heavenly radiance, it takes its first steps towards you.

Hold out your arms to embrace it as it walks to where you are waiting. Let your meeting be a delight and an awakening. The unicorn will allow you to mount its back, for you and this magical being are destined to take many spiritual journeys together, adventuring deep into the heaven worlds.

The unicorn carries you to a place in the wood where you begin to climb upwards. Soon the trees fall away and you are tripping across wild, open moorland. Always you are aware of the unicorn's golden-white horn, going before you like the still, golden-white flame in your heart.

You pass pools surrounded by knotgrass on your upward climb that shake with a strange dark light in which are reflected your own shining soul alight with its flame of spirit, the shining white unicorn, who carries you, and the many faces of the One Great Goddess, who sometimes appears as remote and austere and more often as loving and reassuring. Ravens, curlews, wild geese and lapwings circle and call into the wind.

------

You and the unicorn come upon an ancient grave, a small barrow-mound set in the midst of a stone circle, wild and lonely. The unicorn carries you within. The grave is the mouth of the Underworld.

Together you penetrate the still, deep fastnesses of the Underworld, and you begin to realize in wonder that your Underworld journey is leading you to the Heart of the Holy Mountain, the one you have visited before to sit in contemplation of the Sacred and Eternal Flame.

All the protectors of the inner sanctum of the Holy Mountain allow the unicorn to proceed, for it stands surety for your soul. You come to the chamber where the Holy Flame eternally burns, enshrined in an altar formed from the living rock. Four great guardians stand around it, nature beings that are part god and part angel.

You kneel, the unicorn before you, at the foot of the altar. You see the unicorn take a single gazelle-like spring, and enter the Sacred and Eternal Flame. The horn of the unicorn and the tall, majestic flame become one.

The guardians instruct you and offer their blessings, each in turn.

First, the Guardian of the North steps forward. Listen to his words, receive his blessing. Then the Guardian of the South steps forward. Listen to her words, receive her blessing. Now the Guardian of the East steps forward. Listen to his words, receive his blessing. Lastly, the Guardian of the West steps forward. Listen to her words, receive her blessing.

The guardians silently withdraw, leaving you in adoration of the Sacred and Eternal Flame. The Holy Flame silently scintillates until the flame in your own heart rises and leaps, and you and the Sacred and Eternal Flame become one, linked by your heart.

*The flame in your own heart rises and leaps, and you and the Sacred and Eternal Flame become one, linked by your heart.*

Gradually, the silent flame becomes a blazing star, a perfect Star of Peace, which irradiates every part of the chamber, every part of your being, and shines out with powerful radiance into the world.

You see that every member of humanity, every sentient being on all planes of existence, bathes in the heart-light given out by the flame and enters into a state of peace.

You feel yourself being drawn gently upwards, rising through the air in soul-flight. You pass through the solid rock of the mountain as if it were no more than transparent mist, safe in a channel of spiritual light.

The great sky breaks upon your vision, clear and mystic blue. You are upon the holy mountain top, and above you the immeasurable star gives forth its flood of ineffable love, ineffable power, ineffable peace over all the Earth, silently, magically, eternally.

You know that it shines through you, through your heart-centre; and that, to heal yourself and to heal the world, you have only to link with it consciously and give it forth.

Affirm: *Peace, peace, peace to the world.*

*The star of peace and goodwill shines out over all humanity.*

*The holy balm of peace softly embraces all the Earth.*

When you are ready to return to ordinary consciousness, seal your centres in the usual way. Place the symbol of the bright silver cross in a circle of white light upon your crown, brow, throat, heart and solar plexus.

Alternatively, if you feel the need for a more thorough grounding, earth yourself by making seven sunwise (clockwise) rings of upward-spiralling light, from beneath your feet to above the crown of your head, using your creative imagination. Earth yourself by mentally summoning the light right down through the centre of this spiralling tower of light, actually seeing it go deep into the ground below your feet, rooting you in.

Affirm: *Peace in my heart,*

*Peace in my mind,*

*Peace in my thoughts,*

*Peace in my words,*

*Peace in my actions.*

Go on your way, enlightened by the knowledge that your unicorn will always walk with you, ready to respond to your call when you next wish to meet with it in the exquisite garden at the heart of the magical wood. It will always bring with it joy, delight, guiding wisdom and the balm of peace unbounded from the spirit-worlds, where the star is eternally shining.

## Celtic Blessing

Deep peace of the running wave to you,
Deep peace of the flowing air to you,
Deep peace of the quiet earth to you,
Deep peace of the shining stars to you,
Deep peace of the Son of Peace to you ...

Peace between nations,
Peace between neighbours,
Peace between lovers,
In love of the God of life.

Peace between religions,
Peace between world views,
Peace between differences,
In love of the God of life.

Peace between races,
Peace between man and Earth,
Peace between man and beasts,
In love of the God of life.

Peace between person and person,
Peace between wife and husband,
Peace between parent and child.
In love of the God of life.

The peace of Heaven above all peace.
Bless O Heaven our hearts
Let our hearts incessantly bless,
Bless O Heaven our faces,
Let our faces bless one and all,
Bless O Heaven our eyes,
Let our eyes bless everything they see ...

From the Carmina Gadelica, collected and edited by Alexander Carmichael

# Further Reading

*Ancient Wisdom, Modern World: Ethics for a New Millennium*, His Holiness the Dalai Lama. Little, Brown and Company, 1999

*The Bridge of Stars*, Marcus Braybrooke (General Ed.). Duncan Baird Publishers, 2001

*The Candle of Vision*, A.E. (George William Russell). Prism Press, 1990

*Of Water and the Spirit*, Malidoma Patrice Somé. Arkana, Penguin Books Ltd., 1995

*The Search for the Beloved: Journeys in Sacred Psychology*, Jean Houston. J.P. Tarcher, Inc., 1990

*Shamanic Wisdomkeepers*, Timothy Freke. Godsfield Press Ltd, 1999

*Tao Te Ching*, Lao Tzu. Penguin Classics, Penguin Books Ltd

*Words of Paradise: Selected Poems of Rumi*, Raficq Abdulla. Frances Lincoln Ltd, 2002

The White Eagle Publishing Trust (020 7603 7914)
   White Eagle: *The Book of Starlight / The Lightbringer / The Quiet Mind / The Still Voice*
   Grace Cooke: *Meditation / Sun Men of the Americas*

# Acknowledgements

## AUTHOR'S ACKNOWLEDGEMENTS

Grateful acknowledgement is made for permission to quote the following copyrighted material:

Verses from Krishna's *Dialogue on the Soul*, translated by Juan Mascaró (1962), Penguin Classics 1995; Song of the Sky Loom, published in *World Poetry* (University of Hawaii Press, edited by Catherine Washburne and John S. Major), trans. by Herbert Spindin; Seeking the Beloved, Raficq Abdulla's beautiful poem from his book *Words of Paradise: Selected Poems of Rumi – New Interpretations* (Frances Lincoln, 2000); excerpts from *Sun Men of the Americas*, Grace Cooke, and from the works of White Eagle, reprinted by kind permission of The White Eagle Publishing Trust; special thanks to Lama Khemsar Rinpoche for permission to use his words, derived from an article in *Shamanic Wisdomkeepers* by Timothy Freke (Godsfield Press, 2001), to Malidoma Patrice Somé for the use of his Dagara Prayer, and to Lorraine Mafi-Williams, in respectful memory, for the use of her delightful song, The Mi-Mi Spirits from Space.

Every reasonable care has been taken to trace ownership of copyright material. Information will be welcome which will enable the publisher to correct any reference or credit.

## EDDISON·SADD EDITIONS

EDITORIAL DIRECTOR Ian Jackson
MANAGING EDITOR Tessa Monina
PROJECT EDITOR Jane Laing
PROOFREADER Nikky Twyman
PRODUCTION Karyn Claridge and Charles James

ART DIRECTOR Elaine Partington
PROJECT DESIGNER Hayley Cove
MAC DESIGNER Malcolm Smythe
PICTURE RESEARCHER Diana Morris

Eddison Sadd would like to thank Robert Beer, Megumi Biddle, Garavi Gujarat Newsweekly, Icorec, Jang Publications Ltd and Gila Zur for supplying the script featured in the illustrations. The photograph on page 14 is by Laura Knox.